Lenin

THE IMPORTANCE OF

Lenin

These and other titles are included in The Importance Of biography series:

Maya Angelou	Ernest Hemingway
Louis Armstrong	Adolf Hitler
Neil Armstrong	Thomas Jefferson
Lucille Ball	John F. Kennedy
The Beatles	Martin Luther King Jr.
Alexander Graham Bell	Bruce Lee
Napoleon Bonaparte	John Lennon
Rachel Carson	Abraham Lincoln
Fidel Castro	Charles Lindbergh
Charlie Chaplin	Douglas MacArthur
Charlemagne	Paul McCartney
Winston Churchill	Margaret Mead
Hillary Rodham Clinton	Golda Meir
Christopher Columbus	Mother Teresa
Leonardo da Vinci	John Muir
James Dean	Richard M. Nixon
Charles Dickens	Pablo Picasso
Walt Disney	Edgar Allan Poe
Dr. Seuss	Queen Elizabeth I
F. Scott Fitzgerald	Jonas Salk
Henry Ford	Margaret Sanger
Anne Frank	William Shakespeare
Benjamin Franklin	Frank Sinatra
Mohandas Gandhi	Tecumseh
John Glenn	J.R.R. Tolkien
Jane Goodall	Simon Wiesenthal
Martha Graham	The Wright Brothers
Lorraine Hansberry	Chuck Yeager

THE IMPORTANCE OF

Lenin

by Corinne J. Naden and Rose Blue

LUCENT
BOOKS ®

THOMSON

GALE

San Diego • Detroit • New York • San Francisco • Cleveland • New Haven, Conn. • Waterville, Maine • London • Munich

LIBRARY OF CONGRESS CATALOGING-IN-PUBLICATION DATA

Naden, Corinne J.
    Lenin / by Corinne J. Naden and Rose Blue
        p. cm. — (Importance Of)
    ISBN 1-59018-233-2 (hardback : alk. paper)
    1. Lenin, Vladimir Ilich, 1870–1924—Juvenile literature. 2. Heads of state—Soviet
Union—Biography—Juvenile literature. 3. Revolutionaries—Soviet Union—Biography—
Juvenile literature 4. Communists—Soviet Union—Biography—Juvenile literature. 5. So-
viet Union—History—1917–1936—Juvenile literature. I. Blue, Rose. II. Title. III. Series.
    DK245.L455N27 2004
    947.084′1′092—dc21

                                                                    2003001643

Contents

Foreword   9

Important Dates in the Life of Vladimir Lenin   10

INTRODUCTION
Founder, Leader, and Thinker   12

CHAPTER 1
A Middle-Class Youth   14

CHAPTER 2
The Making of a Revolutionary   24

CHAPTER 3
Exile   35

CHAPTER 4
The Rise of the Bolsheviks   44

CHAPTER 5
The Aftermath of Bloody Sunday   55

CHAPTER 6
War and Revolution   65

CHAPTER 7
The All-Powerful Revolutionary   77

CHAPTER 8
The Last Years   88

Notes   99
For Further Reading   101
Works Consulted   102
Index   104
Picture Credits   111
About the Authors   112

Foreword

THE IMPORTANCE OF biography series deals with individuals who have made a unique contribution to history. The editors of the series have deliberately chosen to cast a wide net and include people from all fields of endeavor. Individuals from politics, music, art, literature, philosophy, science, sports, and religion are all represented. In addition, the editors did not restrict the series to individuals whose accomplishments have helped change the course of history. Of necessity, this criterion would have eliminated many whose contribution was great, though limited. Charles Darwin, for example, was responsible for radically altering the scientific view of the natural history of the world. His achievements continue to impact the study of science today. Others, such as Chief Joseph of the Nez Percé, played a pivotal role in the history of their own people. While Joseph's influence does not extend much beyond the Nez Percé, his nonviolent resistance to white expansion and his continuing role in protecting his tribe and his homeland remain an inspiration to all.

These biographies are more than factual chronicles. Each volume attempts to emphasize an individual's contributions both in his or her own time and for posterity. For example, the voyages of Christopher Columbus opened the way to European colonization of the New World. Unquestionably, his encounter with the New World brought monumental changes to both Europe and the Americas in his day. Today, however, the broader impact of Columbus's voyages is being critically scrutinized. *Christopher Columbus,* as well as every biography in The Importance Of series, includes and evaluates the most recent scholarship available on each subject.

Each author includes a wide variety of primary and secondary source quotations to document and substantiate his or her work. All quotes are footnoted to show readers exactly how and where biographers derive their information, as well as provide stepping-stones to further research. These quotations enliven the text by giving readers eyewitness views of the life and times of each individual covered in The Importance Of series.

Finally, each volume is enhanced by photographs, bibliographies, chronologies, and comprehensive indexes. For both the casual reader and the student engaged in research, The Importance Of biographies will be a fascinating adventure into the lives of people who have helped shape humanity's past and present, and who will continue to shape its future.

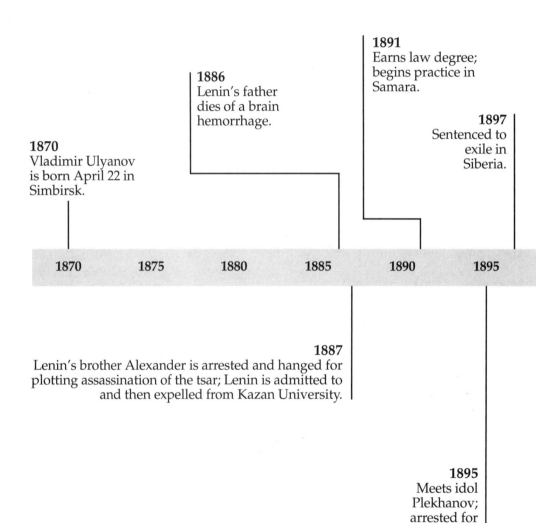

IMPORTANT DATES IN THE LIFE OF VLADIMIR LENIN

1891
Earns law degree;
begins practice in
Samara.

1886
Lenin's father
dies of a brain
hemorrhage.

1897
Sentenced to
exile in
Siberia.

1870
Vladimir Ulyanov
is born April 22 in
Simbirsk.

| 1870 | 1875 | 1880 | 1885 | 1890 | 1895 |

1887
Lenin's brother Alexander is arrested and hanged for
plotting assassination of the tsar; Lenin is admitted to
and then expelled from Kazan University.

1895
Meets idol
Plekhanov;
arrested for
revolutionary
activities.

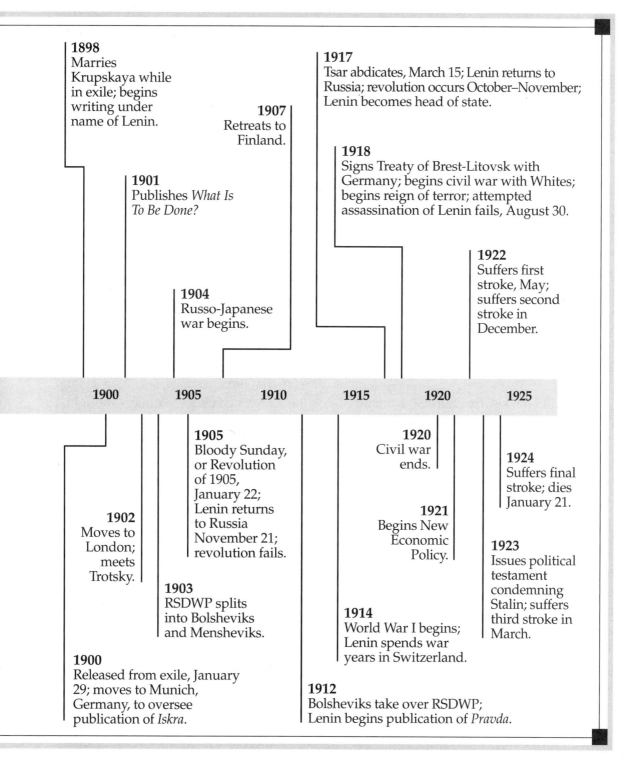

1898
Marries Krupskaya while in exile; begins writing under name of Lenin.

1907
Retreats to Finland.

1917
Tsar abdicates, March 15; Lenin returns to Russia; revolution occurs October–November; Lenin becomes head of state.

1918
Signs Treaty of Brest-Litovsk with Germany; begins civil war with Whites; begins reign of terror; attempted assassination of Lenin fails, August 30.

1901
Publishes *What Is To Be Done?*

1922
Suffers first stroke, May; suffers second stroke in December.

1904
Russo-Japanese war begins.

1900   1905   1910   1915   1920   1925

1905
Bloody Sunday, or Revolution of 1905, January 22; Lenin returns to Russia November 21; revolution fails.

1920
Civil war ends.

1924
Suffers final stroke; dies January 21.

1902
Moves to London; meets Trotsky.

1921
Begins New Economic Policy.

1903
RSDWP splits into Bolsheviks and Mensheviks.

1923
Issues political testament condemning Stalin; suffers third stroke in March.

1914
World War I begins; Lenin spends war years in Switzerland.

1900
Released from exile, January 29; moves to Munich, Germany, to oversee publication of *Iskra*.

1912
Bolsheviks take over RSDWP; Lenin begins publication of *Pravda*.

Founder, Leader, and Thinker

He was born Vladimir Ilich Ulyanov, but the world knows him by just one name—Lenin. Founder of the Russian Communist Party, leader of the Bolshevik Revolution, builder and first head of the Soviet state, Lenin was perhaps the most significant political leader of the twentieth century.

Little in Lenin's early childhood points to the creation of a professional revolutionary. His parents were educated and cultured, his family life happy and closely knit. An outstanding student at the top of his class, he seemed far more destined for a university classroom than for a life of exile, turmoil, and revolution.

But young Vladimir was born in a place and time that was on the brink of change. The time was the late 1800s. The Industrial Revolution, which had started in England a century earlier, had slowly crept across Europe. Workers were leaving the farms for the factories in lands where political leadership encouraged growth and opportunities. These changes were beginning but had yet to make great impact upon eastern European countries.

The late nineteenth century also saw the spread of colonialism, whereby various countries conquered and settled large areas of the world. The United States, Germany, and Japan were emerging expansionist powers. Imperialist Russia joined in the expansionist fever, moving into Siberia, the Caucasus, and Asia as far as the Korean coastline. Political thought was changing, too, throughout Europe. In many countries, the more radical thinkers began to call for reforms, for individual liberties, for workers' rights, and for an end to imperialist and nondemocratic rule.

In Russia, however, beyond the expansionist tactics, the worldwide changes were not so evident. In the late 1800s, Vladimir Ulyanov was born into a country where the tsar was the head of state. The tsar ruled his people but did not represent them in terms of providing for their rights or seeing to their well-being. Even the highly educated and cultured were denied basic civil and political rights. In this time when gathering together in a large crowd could be considered suspicious and cause for expulsion from a uni-

Vladimir Ilich Ulyanov, known simply as Lenin, is one of the most significant political leaders of the twentieth century.

versity, sometimes even the most loyal of Russians began to protest in ways that threatened the government.

Vladimir Ulyanov was deeply affected by his place and time. He saw his older brother executed by the state for threatening the tsar. He lived with the stigma that fell on the family of a state criminal. He suffered his own dismissal from university life and eventual exile to the wasteland of Siberia and then to Europe. Through the years, he developed a social doctrine based upon the thought of Karl Marx, a German economic, social, and political philosopher. Marx held that capitalism, the economic system based on free enterprise, would be replaced by communism, with no private property and no social classes or divisions. Most important, it argued that such a transition could be achieved only by revolution. In time, Lenin's own brand of social order would bring about what some historians have called the most significant political events of the twentieth century—the Russian or Bolshevik Revolution and the creation of the Union of Soviet Socialist Republics.

Lenin may not have caused the revolution in his country, but he rose in importance at just the right time, just as Russia was ready for his leadership. This man became one of history's greatest revolutionary leaders and statesmen.

Chapter

1 A Middle-Class Youth

Vladimir Ulyanov grew up in the cultured, protected home of Russian intellectuals, which seemed a world away from the discontent and injustice that would soon destroy the foundations of his country. He was born in the southern Russian city of Simbirsk (present-day Ulianovsk) on April 22, 1870, to Ilya Nikolayevich Ulyanov and Maria Alexandrovna Ulyanova. His father, Ilya, was an inspector, later a director, of public schools, both prestigious positions. Ilya, the son of a shoemaker, was of Mongolian ancestry, which may have accounted for Lenin's high cheekbones and slightly slanted eyes. Lenin's mother was the daughter of a Jewish doctor from the city of Zhitomir on the Polish border.

A SHELTERED LIFE

The third of six children, Lenin was first taught at home by his mother. When he was five, a tutor came daily to the house, normal practice for a well-off Russian. The boy attended the local school at the age of nine. Early in his schooling years, it was obvious that young Vladimir, called Volodya by the family, was a gifted student.

Said Leon Trotsky in his book on the young Lenin, "Vladimir learned with extraordinary ease. This active and noisy boy with his wide scope of emotions was also capable of truly astounding concentration."[1] As Lenin grew, his school reports continued to praise him. A later report said he was "a walking encyclopaedia, extremely useful to his comrades and the pride of his teachers."[2]

Physically, Lenin was described by a schoolmate as

> rather short but fairly powerfully built, with slightly hunched up shoulders and a large head. . . . Small ears, prominent cheekbones, a short, wide, slightly squashed nose. . . . With no eyebrows on his freckled face, Ulyanov had longish, blond, soft and slightly curly hair which he combed straight back. But all these irregularities were redeemed by his high forehead, under which burned two fierce little brown eyes. His ungainly appearance was easily forgotten in conversation under the effect of these small but unusual eyes which sparkled with extraordinary intelligence and energy.[3]

14 ■ THE IMPORTANCE OF LENIN

In his youth, Lenin seemed destined for an academic life. His good record in school and the fact that, according to his biographers, he was the family favorite gave Lenin a deep sense of self-confidence at an early age. He developed a somewhat superior attitude around his peers and was inclined to be intolerant of their views. Perhaps for that reason, he had no close friends. He spent his time reading or playing with his brothers and sisters.

Lenin's boyhood in Simbirsk, a sleepy town on the Volga River, was apparently quiet and happy within his close and loving family unit. The Ulyanovs were not considered wealthy compared to the very well-off in Russia at the time. But the fact that they had a large home, a garden, a cook, and a handyman put them far above most of Russia's population, some 80 million peasants who lived off patches of land and starved when the harvests were bad. However, the Ulyanovs were considerably below a small number of very rich Russians who lived on grand country estates or in elegant mansions in St. Petersburg or Moscow. And above them all was the country's most wealthy individual, the emperor or tsar.

THE HOUSE OF ROMANOV

Lenin grew up in a land whose tsar was beholden to no one. The ruling family, whom Lenin would become determined to overthrow, was called the House of Romanov, in power since 1613. The tsar in Russia had absolute control. Laws were passed or not passed at the whim of the ruler, and there was no parliament or legislative body to challenge him. Nicholas I, for instance, is called the emperor who froze Russia for thirty years because so little legislation was passed during his reign (1825–1855). Alexander II instituted some liberal reforms in 1861, and on the day he was assassinated in March 1881 he created a number of commissions that might eventually have evolved into a representative parliament. But his conservative son Alexander III canceled many of the

Lenin was the family favorite and a gifted student. He was also extremely self-confident at an early age.

The Ulyanov Family

Lenin's mother and father came from considerably different backgrounds. His father, Ilya Nikolyevich, was of a working-class family and a member of the Russian Orthodox Church. He had moved his own family to Simbirsk shortly before Lenin's birth because he had been appointed inspector of popular schools for the province. The government at the time was pushing a rapid expansion of education in Russia. In such a position, Ilya immediately became a prominent figure in town. Lenin's mother, Maria Alexandrovna Blank, was the daughter of a doctor from a cultured family in Germany. Her grandfather, Moshko Blank, was a Jewish trader. When Maria's father retired from practice, he settled in the family estate at Kokushkino, which Lenin's mother would later inherit.

Lenin's parents raised their children in the church and in Russian culture, counting themselves as loyal subjects of the tsar. Their total commitment was to the education of their children. Eight in all were born into the household: Anna and Alexander followed by Lenin; then Olga, Dmitri, and Maria. Another boy and girl died in infancy, which was not unusual in those times of poor health care standards. Ilya's job often kept him away from home, and Maria assumed complete responsibility for the running of the household and caring for the children. Both parents were quiet, unassuming, respectable, and model members of Russian society in the late 1800s.

The Ulyanovs were a respectable, middle-class family. Lenin (lower right), seen here at age nine, was the third of six children.

reforms of his father. In fact, Alexander III stated that he had no intention of limiting the autocratic, or absolute, power he had inherited. Out of this vast and varied land, he wanted to forge a country of one nationality, one language, one religion, and one form of government—his. To ensure this, he could never allow his citizens free speech or press.

Two Tragedies

The autocratic rule of the tsar was not often a topic of conversation in the Ulyanov home. In fact, Lenin's parents had always been the tsar's most loyal subjects. Like many Russians of the period, they did not doubt the tsar's authority and regarded one's duty as obeying his laws and performing one's work honestly and with pride.

Home life during Lenin's early years was characterized by his parents' devotion to education and strong drive to succeed. His parents, according to one biographer,

> were new Russians in the sense that they were of diverse ethnic ancestry.... Living by the Volga [River] among Russians, the Ulyanovs were a bit like first-generation immigrants. They had a terrific zeal to succeed, and this zeal was passed on to their progeny [children].... They associated themselves with modernity and wanted Russia to become more akin to the countries of the West.[4]

In this atmosphere, Lenin occupied himself with his studies, skating on the frozen river, reading, playing chess, or taking part in his older brother's chemical experiments. Alexander, called Sasha, was a quiet, thoughtful, and intelligent young man who had a great influence on Lenin's early years. They were together a good deal. Lenin missed his brother greatly when Sasha went off to St. Petersburg University to study science.

When Lenin was fifteen years old, the first of two tragic events changed his future. The first was the untimely death of his father, who died of a brain hemorrhage in January 1886 at the age of fifty-five. Shortly before, Ilya had been informed that he was marked for early retirement, possibly because the tsar thought he was spending too much money building new schools and expanding the education program too quickly. Although the family was left with only a small pension, they were able to keep the house and continued to live a fairly comfortable life.

Some reports say that in later years Lenin, who was present when his father died, became an atheist at that time. Lenin himself disliked religious discussions and once wrote, according to Harold Shukman in his book on the revolution, that "this talking about gods and devils instead of attacking all religions, was a hundred times worse than saying nothing at all on the subject."[5] The death of Ilya changed both Lenin and his brother in other ways as well. Sasha, always the most gentle of people, was nearly driven mad with grief, as his sister Anna recounted in her memoirs. He became a harder, more demanding person. As for

Lenin, with his brother away at school, he was now the head of the family and had to help his mother care for the younger children. He showed no resentment about this, and his way of coping with grief and stress was to throw himself more diligently into his studies.

Shocking as was the death of his father, Lenin was even more stunned by the second disaster that so profoundly affected the family. His older brother was arrested in the capital city of St. Petersburg on March 1, 1887, for plotting to kill Tsar

Lenin was shocked when his brother was arrested for plotting to kill Tsar Alexander III (pictured).

Alexander III with a homemade bomb. Anna was visiting Sasha at the time, and she was arrested too. Lenin had not even known his brother thought about politics, let alone planned to overthrow the government. Indeed, Sasha turned out to be the mastermind behind a terrorist plot to assassinate the tsar.

The family assumed that Sasha and his comrades would receive a prison term for their involvement if they pleaded for mercy from the court. Indeed, Lenin's mother traveled to St. Petersburg to try to influence authorities to give her son a reduced sentence. But all those hopes faded when Sasha stated defiantly at his trial that violence and revolution were the only recourse for change in his country.

The Underlying Causes

Although Sasha's involvement in a revolutionary plot was shocking to Lenin, the idea of revolution was not uncommon in Russia during that period. It had been building for a long time. When Alexander II became tsar in 1855, he was well aware that Russia lagged behind the nations of Europe in economics and standard of living. He decided that the first step in reform was to get rid of the ages-old practice of serfdom. At the time, the vast majority of Russia's population was serfs, or slaves. They were the legal property of the noblemen whose estates they worked. The serfs were treated shamefully and barely managed to survive even

REBELLION

Shortly before his execution, Sasha (Alexander) Ulyanov was granted a final meeting with his mother. In his book Black Night, White Snow, *journalist Harrison Salisbury sums up Sasha's view of revolution, which Lenin came to adopt:*

"On April 1, two weeks before delivering his final speech, Ulyanov had been permitted a meeting with his mother, Mariya Alexandrovna. The Czar gave his permission because he thought the interview would reveal to the despairing woman the 'true nature' of her son. A prison official was unobtrusively present. Mother and son wept, Alexander begging his mother to forgive him for bringing her such grief. Then he talked of the dictatorial, repressive regime which held the country in thrall [bondage] and of the duty, as he saw it, of every honest man to fight for the liberation of Russia.

'Yes,' sighed his mother, 'but with such terrible means!'

'But,' replied Alexander in the classic form in which the question had been asked by so many generations of young Russians, '*Chto delat?* What is there to do, Mama, when there are no other means?'"

when harvests were good. Their personal condition was of far less concern to the tsar than the fact that so many of them—some nine hundred thousand—were in his army. He feared that their growing unrest would mean a loss of loyalty to him. Accordingly, the tsar freed the Russian serfs in 1861.

It was not long before the newly freed serfs, now known as peasants, realized they had exchanged one kind of slavery for another—this one financial. With the nobles loath to give up land, the peasants were allotted such small plots that they could hardly feed themselves and their families, and if the harvest failed, they starved. Add to that the taxes and mort-

gages imposed on them by the government and their former owners, and a growing hatred was emerging from the formerly docile serfs against the nobles and the government.

Shortly after the serfs were freed, revolutionary groups began to emerge. One of the outstanding figures was a young socialist writer and economist named Nikolay Gavrilovich Chernyshevsky, who would influence many generations of Russians, including Lenin. Various socialist groups developed. Socialism is a system in which private property and income distribution are controlled by the government in an attempt to make living standards equal for all. These groups

St. Petersburg—The Splendid City

Architecturally one of Europe's most splendid cities and the second-largest city in Russia, St. Petersburg has played a long and vital role in the history of the country and in the life of Lenin. Located on the delta of the Neva River at the head of the Gulf of Finland, it is both a vital seaport/industrial center and a site of great culture.

The city was founded by Peter I, known as Peter the Great, in 1703. It was renamed Petrograd in 1914 and Leningrad, after Lenin's death, in 1924. The original name was restored in 1991.

The most famous historical site in St. Petersburg is the art museum known as the Hermitage, founded by Catherine the Great as a court museum in 1764. Adjoining the Winter Palace of the royal leader, it served as a private gallery for her art collection. It was reconstructed by Nicholas I during 1840–1852 and opened to the public in 1852. The art collections of the tsar became public property after the Russian Revolution of 1917. The Hermitage has an outstanding collection of masterpieces by Renaissance western European as well as Russian artists.

When Lenin moved the Russian capital to Moscow in 1918, the population of what was then Petrograd fell and its industry dwindled, but after a five-year plan begun in 1929, the city prospered once again. St. Petersburg was one of the initial targets of Germany at the beginning of World War II and endured a nine hundred-day siege when Germans blockaded the city. More than six hundred thousand people starved to death. For its heroic stand, St. Petersburg was awarded the Soviet Union's most distinguished medal, the Order of Lenin. However, St. Petersburg did not regain its prewar population until the 1960s and today numbers more than 4 million.

The Hermitage museum is the most famous historical site in St. Petersburg.

wanted to seize power and bring about reforms with varying degrees of violence. However, some reforms were instituted by the worried tsar, and for a while conditions improved for at least a small number of Russians, quieting the talk of revolution.

By 1879, the underground movement had split into two main groups. Black Repartition wanted no terrorism and called for land to be redistributed among the peasants, who were known as "black folks." People's Freedom advocated terrorism against the tsar and government officials as the only way to gain the attention and the support of the populace. In 1881, People's Freedom got everyone's attention by assassinating Alexander II. Alexander III took over the government and was even more oppressive than his father had been. In the following years, Sasha and his comrades planned to use the same tactics of People's Freedom to assassinate Alexander III.

THE CHANGE BEGINS

After a quick trial and sentencing, Sasha was hanged in the courtyard of the Schlusselburg Fortress in May 1887. Although his sister Anna was released, she was forced by the government to live about 150 miles up river from Simbirsk on a small estate at Kokushkino, which her mother had inherited from her own father. Since Anna had been visiting Sasha before his arrest, she was on a list of those who might be engaged in revolutionary activities.

Suddenly at age seventeen, Lenin, still a schoolboy, found himself head of a household that carried the stigma of having reared a state criminal. He was certainly aware that his home and his family would now be watched carefully by the authorities. They were already watched by their neighbors, who suddenly seemed wary of being too friendly with a family of such dubious reputation. These neighbors feared they too might come under the surveillance of government police.

Despite the tragedies, Lenin graduated from high school with great honors and was given a glowing letter of recommendation by his school principal, Fyodor Kerensky, one of the few who did not turn away from the family. Lenin had decided to become a lawyer, and the letter eased his admission as a law student into the imperial Kazan University (now Kazan State University) in the fall of 1887. At this time his mother sold the house in Simbirsk and moved upriver to the estate where Anna was living under police surveillance. After spending his first seventeen years in the security of the family home, Lenin moved to Kazan, but he would spend the next several years of his life never putting down deep roots anywhere.

Serious, reliable, studious, and prompt, Lenin entered Kazan University, but his college career was short-lived. Lenin showed no interest in politics, but his mother, knowing that the authorities would keep an eye on Lenin because of Sasha, made him promise he would stay clear of any political activity. Perhaps he did not regard a student protest meeting

LENIN'S HOMELAND

The land that Lenin spent his adult life trying to change was called Russia before he turned it into the Soviet Union. Since 1991, it has been called Russia once again. The largest country in the world, Russia occupies some 5,592,800 square miles of space in eastern Europe and Asia. It is so huge that it contains every type of climate except the true tropics and spans eleven time zones. Its population today is nearly 145 million.

Russian history dates back to the fifth century when Slavic tribes began migrating into the area. The first Russian state was established in the ninth century by Scandinavian chieftains around present-day Novgorod and Kiev, but the country was overrun by the Mongols in the thirteenth century. By 1480, the grand dukes of Muscovy, or Moscow, freed themselves from Mongol rule, and Ivan the Terrible became Russia's first proclaimed tsar in 1547. Peter the Great founded the Russian Empire in 1721. After the Russian Revolution and the last of the tsars in 1917, Russia became the Union of Soviet Socialist Republics.

Ivan the Terrible was Russia's first proclaimed tsar.

about living conditions as political activity, but he attended one in December mainly out of curiosity. The local police, who feared that such gatherings would spark unrest among the student community, took the names of all who attended.

Even though he was only a spectator at the meeting and had not taken part in it, Lenin was promptly expelled. The official report said, "He attracted attention by his secretiveness, inattentiveness and indeed rudeness."[6]

Lenin's mother was most upset and tried desperately to get the authorities to reinstate her son, to no avail. Not only was he the brother of a convicted state criminal, but Lenin himself was now under suspicion. The authorities were taking no chances. Replied one official to his mother's plea for Lenin's return to the university, "We can scarcely do anything for Ulyanov."[7] The director of the Education Department in St. Petersburg appeared somewhat insulted at the request, declaring, "Isn't this the brother of *that* Ulyanov? . . . Yes, it's clear . . . he certainly should not be admitted."[8] Instead, Lenin was banished to the family home at Kokushkino.

Even with anger and grief over the government's treatment of his brother and himself, at this point Lenin still gave no indication—if he openly discussed such matters at all—of favoring retaliation or change by violent action. His expulsion for a trivial offense would give young Lenin time to think much more seriously about his government's activities as well as the radical ideas that his brother embraced.

2 The Making of a Revolutionary

Lenin's expulsion from Kazan University and his subsequent exposure to the works of various socialist writers began to change the young man's ideas about political activism and the necessity of revolution. He spent the next nine months at Kokushkino living with his mother and his sister Anna. Although he had been expelled and then banished by the government because of suspected involvement in unlawful student activity, life under watchful police eyes was hardly prison. Life was peaceful, if isolated, on the estate. When he was younger and had accompanied his family to Kokushkino, Lenin had enjoyed boat trips on the river and afternoons spent walking through the forest. This stay was somewhat different, however. He spent much of his time reading a wide range of both Russian and Western political literature. According to one biographer, "Vladimir was not particularly unhappy. The house was filled with books belonging to his late uncle and for recreation there was skiing and hunting."[9] He also had time to think about the ideas that had led his brother to join a terrorist group.

THE REVOLUTIONARY THINKERS

One of the first writers that led Lenin on his eventual revolutionary path was Nikolay Gavrilovich Chernyshevsky. His work *What Is To Be Done?* (1863) focused on what he called social and economic evils. Some historians call Chernyshevsky the forerunner of Lenin and say that he not only pointed out the necessity of every thinking person to become a revolutionary, but that he also described the kind of revolutionary, the goals of each revolutionary, and by what method the goals could be reached.

Lenin read many other socialist thinkers such as Karl Kautsky and Carl Clausewitz. Kautsky, leader of the German Socialist Democratic Party, opposed violent revolution. Clausewitz was a Prussian general known mainly for his work *On War*, advocating the concept of total war in which all territory, property, and citizens of the enemy are attacked.

Nothing so profoundly affected Lenin, however, as did the writings of nineteenth-century German economic, social, and political philosopher Karl Marx. Marx contended that the economic system based on the rise and fall of the marketplace and known as capitalism carries the seeds of its own destruction. In the constant battle between capitalists for a greater share of the market, more and more automation is introduced into factories, resulting in less profit for the owners. As lower wages are paid to workers, they will not be able to buy as many goods. The economy will experience recession; the workers will be exploited. Out of this will come economic depression. Finally, Marx said, the workers will revolt.

Capitalism, according to Marx, must eventually be replaced by communism, a system in which there is no private property and no social or class divisions. In theory, every citizen shares in the enjoyment of the common wealth, more or less according to his or her need. Furthermore, claimed Marx, this transition can be achieved in only one way—by revolution. The proletariat, meaning the workers, must take control of the means of production from the bourgeoisie, meaning the capitalists who employ the workers, because those who hold control will not give up that control willingly. As quoted in *Three Who Made a Revolution* by Bertram Wolfe, the Russian Marxists believed Marx demonstrated that "all lands must 'inevitably' go through the various stages from feudalism, through capitalism, to socialism."[10]

Marx indicated not only how but also where the revolution would develop. *U.S. News & World Report* further explained his philosophy:

Marx expected revolution in economically and culturally developed countries, where industrial workers, in the majority, would lead the way. Once started, it would sweep simultaneously across most of the industrial nations. Finally would come the global Utopia that—until now—has been the confidently declared vision of Communist leaders. But Marx was wrong from the start. Instead of industrial Europe, the revolution came in Russia, that most improbable of lands.[11]

Marx's call for revolution attracted Lenin. It was as though this studious young man, who heretofore seemed not to have spent time contemplating the state of his society, were suddenly struck by lightning. He was electrified by Marx's

The writings of philosopher Karl Marx (pictured) profoundly affected Lenin.

message in *Das Kapital*. It told him that here was a new order of society waiting to be created, where workers would be in charge of their own affairs and lead productive lives. Lenin would soon expand upon Marx's theories, which formed the basis of Lenin's entire doctrine. Marx discussed theory; Lenin turned the theory into a workbook.

Lenin was also influenced by the theories of Marx's leading exponent in Russia, Georgy Valentinovich Plekhanov, who spent many years abroad in exile. Plekhanov's two-stage Russian revolution appealed to Lenin. According to the theorist, in the first stage, a revolution against the tsar would set up a democracy in Russia, which would result in the growth of capitalism. In the second stage and under the leadership of a social democratic party, the working class would overthrow capitalism and liberate itself in a socialist revolution.

Socialism is a system in which private property and income are controlled by the government. There are many different forms, depending on how much control is exercised. The result is a classless society. Each worker contributes according to skill and takes according to need, more or less. But Marx, and eventually Lenin and other Russian socialists, used the word *communism* to describe this classless society. Indeed, the Communist League was founded in 1847 to distinguish it from other socialist parties.

PURSUING THE LAW

Months after his exile, late in 1888, Lenin was allowed to return to Kazan to live, but he could not reenter the university. He requested permission to study abroad, but that, too, was denied. Near the end of 1890, however, he was given permission

LENIN'S HATRED OF OLD RUSSIA

Following Sasha's execution and Lenin's expulsion from Kazan University, Lenin developed a hatred for his government. While he disagreed with many of the tsar's policies, class bias became one of Lenin's major objections. After working with poor peasants, Lenin realized the problem was more prevalent than he had thought. As a result, Lenin began to vehemently oppose the class system. In *Lenin: A Biography*, author Robert Service says that Lenin despised "every social prop of the tsarist political order. He detested the whole Romanov family, the aristocracy, the clergy, the police and the high command. He hated . . . the middle class."

THE MASTER

The man who most influenced Lenin in political outlook was a nineteenth-century European socialist named Karl Heinrich Marx (1818–1883). More than any other, his writings first opened new avenues of political philosophy to the young Russian. Marx, a theorist and economist, was born in the Rhine province of Prussia and studied at the universities of Bonn and Berlin. A political liberal, he first considered journalism as a career. His *Economic and Philosophical Manuscripts*, written in 1844, show an aversion to anything that impairs individual liberty.

With his wife, Jenny von Westphalen, daughter of a high government official, Marx moved to Paris and established a lifelong friendship with Friedrich Engels. In 1848, Marx and Engels collaborated on *The Communist Manifesto*, which summarizes their entire philosophy. It was published on the eve of the 1848 revolution in France.

The atmosphere in Germany made it possible for Marx to return in 1848 and revive an earlier newspaper in Cologne, but he was expelled again in 1849. He spent the rest of his life studying at the British Museum in London. His most important and best-known work, *Das Kapital*, was published in 1867 and contains his analysis of the economics of capitalism.

from officials in St. Petersburg to study for the law exam on his own. He could not attend lectures, presumably because the officials did not want him to mingle with other students, and he had to teach himself from books. Remarkably, especially considering this handicap, Lenin took less than a year to finish a four-year course and graduated at the top of what would have been his class in November 1891. He received the highest academic degree from the St. Petersburg Board of Education.

Over some police objections, Lenin was admitted to the bar and began to practice law in Samara (now Kuybyshev), where he and his mother had moved in 1889. He worked mainly with poor peasants, and Lenin soon acquired a distaste for his profession because of its great class bias in treating clients. Increasingly, he began to acquire a distaste for social classes in general. However, Lenin continued his work in Samara for two years to please his mother, who was terrified that her second son, now showing the same political leanings as his brother, would become involved in illegal activities. During his spare time, he translated Marx's *The Communist Manifesto* and also read *The Condition of the Working Class in England* (1845) by

Friedrich Engels. At this time, Lenin might not yet have considered himself a full-fledged revolutionary, but he certainly had become a follower of Karl Marx's ideas.

Lenin took some time from his work and readings to join study groups of other socialists who were growing ever more discontented with their country's economic and political systems. But in a short time, he began to have serious disagreements with them, and these disagreements would lead him to shape his own doctrine.

Lenin, seen here at twenty-one years old, taught himself the law from books and was admitted to the bar in 1891.

The disagreement emerged over the terrible famine that Russia suffered in 1891. Soup kitchens and other forms of relief were immediately set up by various socialist groups to aid the starving peasants. Despite the fact that he seemed to espouse blatant cruelty to the poor, Lenin strongly disagreed with any form of aid. Any event or action, such as a famine, that could bring down the existing governmental structure of Russia was good as far as Lenin was concerned. The more disasters that occurred and the more damage they inflicted, the quicker would come the inevitable revolution. Famine, reasoned Lenin, was not an act of fate or nature, but plainly the outcome of a flawed capitalist system. A comrade said some years later, "The gravest, the deepest difference on which we opposed ourselves to Vladimir Ulyanov turned about the attitude to take to the famine of 1891–92."[12]

THE PATH IS CHOSEN

Lenin went to St. Petersburg in August 1893, where he would begin his true life's work. He was twenty-three years old, already bald with a small mustache and beard. Said one biographer,

> There was, he thought, no hope for the country unless industrial and educational progress could be maintained—and St. Petersburg was the vanguard of that movement. He hated Old Russia [the land of the tsar]. . . . What especially attracted him to the capital were not its hundreds of thousands of factory work-

ers but the little group of young Marxist authors who published on the Russian economy and society.[13]

Taking work as a public defender, Lenin traveled about the capital's poorest districts to check on the conditions in which people lived and worked. Sometimes he wore disguises because he was aware that police spies were keeping track of his whereabouts. Russia's proletariat was small compared to its great number of peasants, who were not considered proletariat because they did not have the means of production. But Lenin was convinced that the proletariat, not the peasants, was where the revolution would be waged and won. These Russians—the industrial workers in the cities and towns scattered across the vast land—would become the force that eventually would overthrow the tsar. But first they must come to realize that their own freedom lay in the path to revolution.

Within months Lenin was making a name for himself among the socialists as a leading exponent of revolution. He unified various Marxist groups in the capital into an organization called the Union for the Struggle for the Liberation of the Working Class. He organized cells, groups of six workers to be in charge of distributing pamphlets or creating disturbances against the government at their workplaces. Each group was kept secret from the other so that the whole system would not collapse if one were uncovered. Any messages to and from the cells concerning dates of secret rallies were either in code or written in invisible ink.

BUILDING A REPUTATION

By this time, Lenin was becoming a well-known figure in activist circles because he organized cells and wrote antigovernment pamphlets. His leadership qualities were evident. He was personally charming with a quick understanding of who would be most helpful to him. He had a sense of who could best serve as speechwriters or rally organizers, for example.

Lenin was a man who could not be swayed from his beliefs. Insight into the man appeared in an article in the *New Statesman*, which said,

> He was an arch-schemer, planning his way to his goal, but little diverted by the personal weaknesses that have so often proved stumbling blocks to revolutionary leaders. His chief weakness lay in his intolerance of those who disagreed with him or whom he did not understand—and they were many. Yet that weakness was also in one sense his strength, for it kept him firm in his purpose. Eventually, Lenin would come to dream of a world revolution that would overthrow capitalism in every country. But that part of the dream, which consisted of regenerating Russia and making her a leader in revolutionary thought and the pattern of a developing Socialist state, was not unattainable.[14]

Lenin had now become totally dedicated to the cause of revolution.

At one of his St. Petersburg meetings in 1894, Lenin met another dedicated activist

WIFE AND HELPER

The woman who married Lenin and was by his side through all the political events of his life was Nadezhda Konstantinovna Krupskaya, a Marxist activist. She was plain in appearance, often pictured as not particularly attractive because of bulging eyes due to a thyroid condition. Yet she possessed an active intelligence and an amazing organizing ability, which was of tremendous use to Lenin throughout his life.

Krupskaya came from a family of gentry status, although not so well off as Lenin's. Her father had been an imperial army officer and the family moved frequently. When she reached St. Petersburg, she became acquainted with the ideas of Karl Marx and thereafter made the decision to become a revolutionary, a fact that attracted Lenin to her in the first place.

Much has been said in books about Lenin concerning the lack of genuine love between him and his wife. Whether that is true or not, there was indeed a strong bond between them, which lasted throughout his life. A man as impatient as Lenin needed a partner with extreme patience to see him through the difficult times, and Krupskaya was just that person.

Lenin's wife, Nadezhda Konstantinovna Krupskaya, was an intelligent and extremely patient person.

and his future wife, Nadezhda Konstantinovna Krupskaya. A quote in Clark's biography of Lenin described her in this way:

Krupskaya wanted to . . . [retain] an air of middle-class respectability. Judging by her pictures, her dress in those years was invariably a dark, long-sleeved affair, with very little shape except for slightly puffed-out shoulders and upper arms and a collar of the same stuff that pretty well covered her throat. Her luxuriant hair, parted a little off the middle, was drawn straight back, both neat and austere. Far from seeming drab to Lenin, it is fair to guess that Krupskaya's conservative style was just right for his taste.[15]

Their relationship grew from a casual friendship into love. The union rested in large part on Krupskaya's amazing organizing ability, which became so invaluable to Lenin, especially in his later activities. She would be at his side throughout his life in all his political undertakings and became his most indispensable comrade and secretary.

Also in 1894, Lenin began to disagree with the majority of Russian socialists on the question of the Russian peasants. The members advocated against a Marxist revolution, saying it would not work in Russia because there was practically no proletariat to revolt. They held that socialism would come about through the peasants themselves, but Lenin disagreed. He argued that even if all Russian land could somehow be distributed among all the peasants, the result would not be socialism but capitalism. If the market system and private ownership could not be abolished, declared Lenin, there could be no revolution and no socialism.

By 1894 there were a few signs that a working class was taking some shape in Russia. Industrialism was advancing as railways reached throughout the vast country. As the mining industry grew with the aid of the railroads, other industries slowly developed. All this activity tended to produce a working-class population.

As Lenin's writing and philosophy became more and more activist and revolutionary, his personal life remained conservative. Said one biographer,

> Nor had his childhood quirks vanished. Pencils were still kept (mercilessly) sharp and his desk remained smartly arranged; he cleaned it daily. He also detested waste. When he received letters with blank spaces, he cut off and kept the unused parts. He was careful with his money. . . . Always he drained articles in his neat longhand.[16]

The only thing Lenin was careless about, apparently, was his health. Reportedly, he was too engrossed in work to stick to a well-balanced diet: As a result, he suffered chronic stomach problems, an ulcer, headaches, and sleeplessness.

AN UNEXPECTED JOURNEY

In March 1895, for no discernible reason, the Russian Ministry of the Interior dropped its objections to granting Lenin a passport. For some time he had wanted to travel in Europe, mostly to see his idol, Plekhanov, but the government had always refused his requests due to his revolutionary activity. Now twenty-five years old, Lenin left in late April on a four-month journey. His first stop was Moscow, where he met an old friend newly released from prison and sent his mother a postcard as he had promised. He crossed into Switzerland and found the Alps enchanting but was forced to see a doctor because of his recurring stomach problems. The doctor told him to stop eating oily foods and to drink mineral water.

The End of the Line

Much of Lenin's hatred for autocratic rule centered on Nikolay Aleksandrovich, last in the line of the three hundred-year-old House of Romanov and eldest son of Alexander III. Born in 1868 in Tsarskoye Selo near St. Petersburg, he ascended the throne upon the assassination of his father and was crowned in Moscow in 1896. From his earliest years, Nicholas was ill suited to the complex tasks he would face as the leader of a vast empire in a troubled time. Trained for the military, he delighted in the sporting contests of young army officers of his day and had little appetite for intellectual pursuits. A charming young man, Nicholas was in fact rather shy and ill at ease in formal occasions.

Nicholas was passionately devoted to his wife Alexandra, whom he married in 1894. With a far stronger character than Nicholas possessed, Alexandra dominated her husband, and he took her advice on spiritualists and faith healers.

Tsar Nicholas had a simple view of his role as head of Russia. His power came from God and, therefore, the tsar was responsible to no one *but* God. In addition, he distrusted his ministers and rarely listened to them, perhaps because he felt intellectually inferior. He constantly worried that they were trying to take away his power. But even with a conviction that his was the only rule in Russia, he lacked the strength of will to lead and fought internal wars with himself when faced with decisions. With Russia ripe for revolution and with a man such as Lenin spearheading the drive, it is doubtful that any tsar could have withstood him or the force of the revolution, but certainly Nicholas II was no match for either one.

Tsar Nicholas II believed he answered to no one but God.

Next, Lenin rented an apartment in Paris for a time, and from there he want back to Switzerland and finally to Berlin, where he ran out of money. His mother sent him some funds. He bought a small present in Berlin for his sister Maria, and supposedly that was the last she ever got from him except for copies of the books he wrote.

The highlight of Lenin's trip abroad was a meeting with Plekhanov in Geneva. Apparently, the two men got along well and Lenin informed Plekhanov of the latter's growing support in the Russian capital.

Back home in St. Petersburg in late September, Lenin told his comrades of the contacts he had made during his trip and also stepped up his revolutionary activities. He wrote inflammatory pamphlets and got them distributed among workers, which helped to bring on a series of factory strikes. Because of his actions, he was sentenced to jail in December.

Jail Time

Imprisonment for Lenin came as an unpleasant shock because he knew that the Okhrana, the Russian secret police, had always regarded him and his comrades as too intellectual to cause much trouble beyond writing pamphlets and giving speeches. But when the police got word of some of the underground work of the Union for the Struggle for the Liberation of the Working Class, something had to be done. Lenin was interrogated before imprisonment but prided himself on not giving out any information.

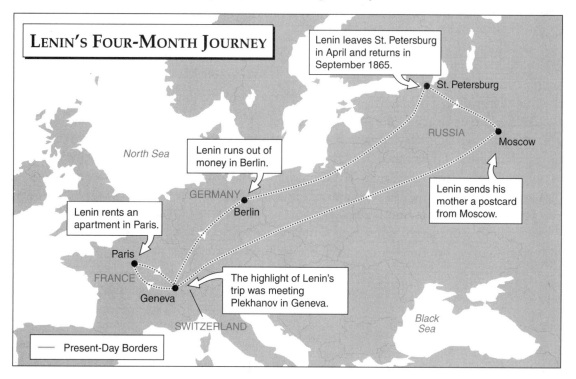

LENIN'S FOUR-MONTH JOURNEY

Lenin leaves St. Petersburg in April and returns in September 1865.

St. Petersburg

RUSSIA

Moscow

North Sea

Lenin runs out of money in Berlin.

GERMANY

Berlin

Lenin sends his mother a postcard from Moscow.

Lenin rents an apartment in Paris.

Paris

FRANCE

Geneva

The highlight of Lenin's trip was meeting Plekhanov in Geneva.

SWITZERLAND

Black Sea

— Present-Day Borders

Lenin's jail time in cell 193, the House of Preliminary Detention, St. Petersburg, lasted fourteen months, from December 1895 until February 1897. Considering that his antigovernment activities were by now well known to police, his imprisonment was relatively easy. When he was sent to prison, his mother and Anna moved to St. Petersburg from Moscow where they had been living. Anna brought books to his cell and took out coded messages urging others in the Union to keep up the agitation in the factories. According to Hill, Lenin "continued to produce pamphlets and proclamations, writing them in milk, using 'inkwells' made of bread which could be swallowed if necessary."[17] He was allowed visitors twice a week and also began work on his first full-length book, *The Development of Capitalism in Russia* (published in 1899). He also polished his own cell floor because he thought it was a good form of exercise to keep himself in shape. All in all, he passed the time productively and almost comfortably.

While Lenin was serving time in jail, he was not the only Ulyanov in trouble with the tsarist regime. His brother Dmitri was expelled from Moscow University and banished to Tula for his involvement in revolutionary activities. His sister Maria was arrested for the same offense and sent to Nizhni Novgorod. But Lenin's mother soon persuaded the authorities to release both of them to the house she had rented in Podolsk south of Moscow. Anna and her husband were already living there.

It is said at this time that Lenin's mother was showing signs of mental strain. One of Lenin's biographers dryly remarked,

> She had also been suffering from a stomach ailment. One of the doctor's questions was whether she had suffered recent 'spiritual disturbances.' A more tactless enquiry is hard to imagine. Maria Alexandrovna's [Mrs. Ulyanov's] husband had died prematurely. Her eldest son had been hanged. Three other children had been arrested. . . . She had long since stopped dreaming that her family would continue along the normal paths of their professional careers. Each year seemed to bring a fresh crop of trouble to the Ulyanovs. No wonder Maria Alexandrovna showed signs of strain.[18]

Although Lenin himself showed no outward signs of strain, he was well aware that his easy jail sentence was unlikely to last. Clearly the government still felt threatened by him, for in February 1897 he was banished to the eastern Russian province of Siberia for a period of three years.

Chapter

3 Exile

Lenin spent the first part of his three-year exile in Siberia adjusting to his strange surroundings and the rest of his time writing on the failures of capitalism and developing his theory of a socialist state. At the time of Lenin's arrest, nearly all members of the Union had also been jailed and they, too, were banished. Called administrative exile, it was banishment without trial or recourse to the courts, and it worked on a graded system. The more dangerous the criminal was to the state, the farther away he or she would be sent. Good behavior was assured because misdeeds would result in more distant or perhaps permanent banishment or worse living conditions. This type of exile to remote parts of Russia was usually given to those people whose activities, such as joining Marxist groups or promoting strikes and demonstrations, the government found suspicious.

Interestingly, given Lenin's obvious participation in so-called suspicious behavior and Marxist groups, the tsarist government was remarkably lenient about his exile. Russian writer Fyodor Dostoyevsky in 1861–1862 published *The House of the Dead*, which was a vivid account of his own period of Siberian exile in 1850. Dostoyevsky spoke of the prison in Omsk where he spent four years at hard labor, working in chains and enduring barbaric living conditions. However, said a Lenin biographer,

> Savage floggings and arbitrary killings such as Dostoyevsky had witnessed during his Siberian exile in the Fifties were things of the past. Here and there in Siberia were to be found prisons where tyrannical warders ruled ... but a revolutionary who called for the destruction of the social order could expect to be treated as an intellectual and provided with all the necessities of life. If he had money, he could live exactly as he had lived in European Russia. . . . His punishment was that he was separated from the great cities, and for many revolutionaries in need of rest and leisure to think out their revolutionary programs, exile was more a blessing than a punishment.[19]

Lenin spent three days before his departure meeting with other members of the Union. Obviously, their dreams of revolution were on hold, but all promised they would sit out their banishment terms without trying to escape. Lenin left

Like Lenin, Fyodor Dostoyevsky was banished to Siberia. The author published a book detailing his experiences there.

St. Petersburg on February 17, 1897, after posting a letter, partly in invisible ink, to Krupskaya asking her to marry him.

At his mother's request, citing her son's poor health, Lenin was allowed to go to Siberia without police guard and at his own expense, which meant he could travel in comfort. His mother and sisters Anna and Maria even traveled with him for the first part of the journey. Lenin was alone for the remainder of the trip.

To Shushenskoye

Lenin's impressions of Siberia are vivid in this excerpt from a letter to his mother:

> The country covered by the West Siberian Railway that I have just travelled throughout its entire length . . . is astonishingly monotonous—bare, bleak steppe [vast tracts of level, treeless land]. No sign of life, no towns, very rarely a village or patch of forest—and for the rest, all steppe. Snow and sky—and nothing else for the whole three days.[20]

In Krasnoyarsk in central Siberia, Lenin was delayed for two months due to blizzards. The authorities there seemed not to have the slightest idea what to do with him, so Lenin was left pretty much on his own. He stayed in the home of a woman noted for her sympathy to revolutionaries and passed some time in the well-stocked library of a wealthy merchant just outside of town.

In spring, Lenin was relocated to Shushenskoye, a village of about fifteen hundred inhabitants in the vast, largely desolate region of northeastern Russia. He arrived in late April. Although the weather in Siberia—where temperatures have been known to reach ninety below zero—was harsh, life in Shushenskoye was not too much of a hardship for Lenin. In fact, considering other possibilities, he was quite pleased with his new home. The village lay on a tributary of the Yenisei, near forests and in sight of the Sayan Mountains. Hunting was good and food was cheap. No one asked him to do any work. He was under no restraints. He was allowed to visit others who had been exiled and hold meetings. He could even entertain his relatives if they chose to visit.

Lenin found lodging in the house of a moderately well-off peasant, who built shelves in his room to accommodate the books that were sent from Lenin's mother and sister. In fact, Lenin's main complaint was that books did not arrive quickly enough.

In Siberia, companionship was precious. The problem for most exiles was loneliness. After several months, one of Lenin's comrades could bear it no longer and shot himself. Lenin took control of his situation and dealt with his own loneliness in a different way. He wrote a letter to the St. Petersburg Police Department in January 1898, asking that his fiancée be allowed to join him.

LENIN'S MARRIAGE

Nadezhda Krupskaya—whom Lenin called Nadya—was already in exile, for the same reason as her fiancé, when his proposal for marriage arrived. She was serving her time in Ufa in the southern Urals. However, the authorities agreed to relocate her to be with Lenin on the condition that the two marry soon after her arrival. Lenin was impatient to see her, partly because

MODIFYING MARX

Lenin recognized the need to alter Karl Marx's theory of revolution before it could be applied to Russia. In the book Russia: 1917–1964, *author J.N. Westwood explains,*

"What Lenin brought to the Russian marxists was a modification of doctrine to make Marxism more suitable for Russian conditions, and the concept of a select and professionalized party, single-minded and able, if necessary, to act decisively without the support of public opinion. He incorporated into Marxist doctrine the possibility of one social class making not one, but two, revolutions. This concept at once enabled Marxists to expect a workers' revolution in their own lifetime. It also gave a place to Russia's dominant social class, the peasantry; for in the first—bourgeois—revolution envisaged by Lenin the bourgeois attack on the monarchy was to be stimulated and largely executed by the proletariat acting in alliance with the peasants. In the second revolution the proletariat would overthrow the bourgeoisie, again with the help of the peasantry."

she was bringing a whole library of books. Krupskaya arrived in Shushenskoye on May 6, 1898, accompanied by her mother.

The wedding, however, did not take place until July due to several difficulties. Lenin had to apply to the authorities for the necessary papers because Nadya's mother insisted on a full religious ceremony. Despite the fact that Lenin, now twenty-eight, and Krupskaya, twenty-nine, were atheists, they agreed. The bureaucratic process in Old Russia took nearly two months. Then there was a problem with locating wedding rings. Lenin seemed surprised that the local priest insisted he have them. An exiled comrade who was learning the jeweler's trade came to the rescue with a ring for each of them. Finally, on July 10, 1898, Lenin and Krupskaya were married in a modest ceremony with her mother present and two local peasants serving as witnesses.

The couple and her mother moved into a larger house. Although Lenin seemed genuinely fond of his mother-in-law, she was a deeply religious woman with a tart tongue and the two had many arguments on the subject of religion, which usually ended with Lenin giving up and leaving the room. He often went to his study, which was filled with books sent from his family. He employed a young Siberian girl especially to help with the cooking,

Lenin and Nadya married in 1898 and remained together until Lenin's death in 1924.

since the food Krupskaya prepared was sometimes less than desirable. In turn, she taught the young girl to read and write.

A highly intelligent, hardworking woman, described as rather plain, Krupskaya "enriched his life by serving as wife, secretary, housekeeper, and devoted disciple."[21] Because she was unable to have children, the couple remained childless. Krupskaya stood by Lenin throughout his life, and their affection for each other grew into a stronger bond through the years. But Krupskaya would soon fade into the background of Lenin's revolutionary activities.

After the wedding, Lenin and his wife settled down to a fairly normal routine. They spent their time translating Sidney and Beatrice Webb's *History of Trade Unionism* (1894). The Webbs were socialist economists who deeply affected British radical thought and institutions during the early twentieth century. Cofounders of the London School of Economics and Political Science, they were pioneers in social and economic reforms.

In his spare time, Lenin gave legal counsel to the local citizens, a practice that was actually forbidden while in exile. He even won a case for one of the local miners. However, the government seems to have ignored the fact that he practiced law, perhaps because Shushenskoye was just too far away from the capital to matter to the tsar.

Lenin also had some time for recreational activities. He asked his mother to send him a chess set from home. Long an ardent chess player, he found several partners while in exile and even carried on a long-distance chess match via letter with an acquaintance in another part of Siberia. In Krupskaya's letters written to Lenin's mother, she speaks of the chess games as well as skating on the frozen river and group sings with other neighbors and exiles. Lenin also enjoyed the company of his dog, a setter named Zhenka who followed him when hunting or fishing.

The government also seemed relaxed about rules when it came to matters of health. After Lenin complained about his teeth, he was allowed to travel to Krasnoyarsk, more than a day's journey away, to see a dentist. He spent about two weeks there one mid-August having his teeth worked on and playing chess.

THE EXILE AT WORK

In the last year of his exile, due to end on January 29, 1900, Lenin began his serious plans for the future. With the completion of *The Development of Capitalism* (written as Vladimir Ilin and completed in 1899), he expanded upon Plekhanov's assertion that capitalism was beginning in Russia, signified by better agricultural equipment and a better standard of living for some of the peasants. Lenin said capitalism was already there and pointed out several factors for his claim. Said one of his biographers,

> To those who thought about politics, it was evident what he was up to. If Russia was already a capitalist country, then the time was long overdue for the removal of the Romanov monarchy. A

capitalist country needed political democracy and general civil rights. Tsarism was obsolete. Furthermore, the advanced condition of Russian capitalism meant that it would not be long after the "bourgeois-democratic" revolution against the Romanovs that a second, even deeper revolution could be attempted: socialist revolution. Ulyanov had issued an economic treatise which, he hoped, would attract thousands of converts to the Marxist cause in Russia.[22]

In a sense, social democracy in Russia had taken a step closer to reality a year earlier. In March, three members of the Jewish Workers' Alliance and six Russian Social Democrats attended a conference in the western city of Minsk. They formed an alliance known as the Russian Social Democratic Workers' Party (RSDWP), but they were arrested shortly after their first meeting. Their manifesto was the endorsement of revolution in two stages: first, the overthrow of the tsar by the bourgeoisie and, second, the assumption of government by the proletariat. The RSDWP stressed that the leadership role in the first revolution would be taken over by the workers because the bourgeoisie lacked the strength for it. Although the founders never had a chance to lead the party because they were all arrested, the RSDWP would grow into Russia's most important revolutionary group, largely because of Lenin's eventual leadership.

Lenin got word of the beginnings of this organization and was naturally drawn to it. Even in exile, he was becoming a public figure and a looming presence in the world of those who sought a revolution in Russia. He published articles in socialist journals without repercussion because the government either did not know of these or did not consider them harmful. He studied Marx and Engels and Kautsky. He had begun to attack those who differed from Plekhanov's view that the revolution would occur in two stages.

However, from his place of exile, Lenin was disturbed by the writings of two other activists. One was Eduard Bernstein of the German Social Democratic Party, then the largest and most powerful of Europe's socialist groups. Bernstein contended in his *Evolutionary Socialism* (1899) that socialism could be realized by evolution, not revolution. With more political rights and economic reform, the workers would gradually change the system. Lenin was furious at what he considered the falseness of this reasoning and decided that when he was freed from exile, he would begin a newspaper to counteract what he believed was slovenly thinking.

The other activist who highly incensed Lenin was Pyotr Berngardovich Struve, a liberal Russian political scientist. Struve's book, *Critical Notes on the Economic Development of Russia* (available in Russia in 1894), pictured a gradual change from capitalism to socialism by means of continuing reforms, an idea Lenin opposed. Now, Lenin was furious to learn that Struve, who had written the first manifesto for the RSDWP, called for a complete revision of all Marxist economic theory. He was even more furious to hear that Struve's ideas were gaining some accep-

ICEBOX OF THE WORLD

For decades, scores of Russians who had offended the government in some way were shuffled off to the lonely wastes of what is by far the country's largest and coldest region—Siberia. It stretches forty-three hundred miles from the Urals in the west to the Pacific mountain ranges in the east and extends twenty-two hundred miles from the Arctic Ocean to the Mongolian frontier and the steppes of Kazakhstan. It takes up 2,500,000 square miles, or 30 percent of all Russian territory. Because Siberia is so vast, the climate varies a good deal. The average January temperature in the north is minus eighteen degrees Fahrenheit and a cozier three degrees Fahrenheit in the south. In July, the north warms up to thirty-seven degrees, whereas the south averages out at a more normal seventy-three degrees.

Siberia may seem like the icebox of the world, but it is a rich one. Under the ground can be found about 90 percent of all Russian coal resources, about half of the natural gas, and healthy deposits of iron, ores, and minerals. In addition to the wealth of fur-bearing animals in the forests, Siberia has about two-thirds of Russian timber and thousands of square miles of pasturelands. It does not, however, have a lot of people. For its vast size, Siberia has a population of only about 25 million, or about five people per square mile. Not surprisingly, most of them live in the southern regions.

The Trans-Siberian Railway, the only transportation system in parts of Siberia, is the longest continuous railroad system in the world, covering six thousand miles, or about one-third of the globe. Just getting across Russia requires seven days of train travel, but the train stops several times a day to let the passengers walk around on frozen tundra for a few minutes.

tance among Social Democrats in Russia and western Europe. Such a direction, Lenin believed, would strip the movement of its revolutionary bent.

THE NAME

It was common in Russia in that period for political activists to use aliases. This made it more difficult for the Russian police to keep up with the whereabouts of various marked people. Vladimir Ulyanov began writing under the name Lenin before he left Siberia. The name appeared in print for the first time in a letter sent to Plekhanov in January 1901. It was still later that he used the name in public and perhaps more than a year after that, he was commonly known as Lenin. The name was taken from the longest of the Siberian rivers, the Lena, which travels 2,648 miles from Lake Baikal to the Laptev Sea. Supposedly, he had wanted to use "Volgin," for the Volga River near his childhood home, but Plekhanov had already taken that.

THE DEPARTURE

Although Lenin's term of exile had not been extended, which often happened for some real or imagined infraction, he was still bound by certain rules after his exile ended on January 29, 1900. He could not live in a Russian metropolitan center or university town or in a large industrial city. Outside of that, he was more or less free. However, it was evident that the au-

thorities had no intention of losing track of him. When his mother spoke to the police in St. Petersburg about where he might live, she was told, "You can be proud of your offsprings: one has been hanged already and the rope is waiting for the other."[23]

With his exile over, Lenin left Siberia on February 10, along with his wife, mother-in-law, and some five hundred books packed in boxes. They traveled to Minusinsk, then down the Yenisei River, by horse-drawn cart to Achinsk, and finally took a train to Ufa, where he left Krupskaya to spend the remainder of her sentence—one year—in exile. Lenin was most anxious to get on with his plans for revolution, and apparently neither he nor Krupskaya considered that he should remain in Ufa until both were

THE RIVER OF HIS NAME

When Lenin first thought about using a pen name for his writings, he wanted to take it from the Volga River. But since that was already in use, Lenin took his pen name from the Lena River, a major waterway of Russia and one of the world's longest. It flows some twenty-seven hundred miles from its source in a small mountain lake near Lake Baikal in Central Asia to its mouth on the Arctic Laptev Sea. The Lena, whose name in Yakut means "big river," has three distinct sections, each about nine hundred miles long. From its headwaters to the Vitim River, the Lena flows through a deep-cut valley; in the middle section the valley broadens and crosses a floodplain; in the last section to the sea the valley narrows to only the width of a mile. Along the shores of the Lena are farms and small industrial centers. Russians primarily live there along with Yakuts, a Turkic-speaking people, and other small groups.

free to go. However, he did stay a few days to make sure his wife and her mother were settled.

Interestingly enough, Lenin would become so immersed in revolution that, according to one biographer, Siberia seems to have faded from his mind. Robert Payne noted, "In 1921 he was asked to fill a questionnaire where there was one question: Where have you lived in Russia? He answered: 'Only on the Volga and in the capital states.' It was as though Shushenskoye . . . had never been."[24]

Now thirty years old, Lenin had far to go before his dream would be realized. After three years of austere living, he emerged from Siberia as a dedicated and determined political leader with a cause from which he would not be swayed. Whereas his parents had been committed to Old Russia, Lenin had become committed to forging a New Russia born of revolution.

4 The Rise of the Bolsheviks

Now out of exile, Lenin planned to control a professional party that would lead the revolution. He saw the Russian Social Democratic Workers' Party that had been formed in March 1899 as a beginning. The first step toward his goal was to organize a newspaper that would carry the message of the RSDWP and become a voice for the workers.

Abiding by his restrictions, Lenin chose to live in Pskov, where he had never been before, because it was only about one hundred miles from St. Petersburg. Then he settled down to much the same life he had led before exile—underground activist activity and dodging the police. But his main work was making plans for the illegal newspaper. Toward that end, in early March he slipped into St. Petersburg, which was forbidden, to meet activist Vera Zasulich, who had been sent by Plekhanov. The meeting went well, but in June when Lenin, with his friend Y.O. Martov, again entered the city to distribute illegal literature, they were seized by the police and held for ten days.

Lenin was freed without further restrictions, but it was now clear that he could not hope to continue his work in Russia. And so, after a trip to see his wife in Ufa,

he took a train to Switzerland in August 1900 to meet with Plekhanov.

THE SPARK

It had long been decided that the revolutionary newspaper was to be called *Iskra (The Spark)*, but almost from the start Lenin and Plekhanov, whom he had so much admired, disagreed bitterly. It was mainly a question of who would control the paper and what its aim would be. Plekhanov, acting much like the commander of the group, saw himself as the director of policy, with Lenin as merely an assistant. But Lenin regarded himself as the main director. Plekhanov saw *Iskra* as a tool that would merely encourage people to think about new ideas. Lenin saw it as a practical means that would persuade people to act and reorganize the party. The extent of his anger can be seen in what he wrote about himself and comrade Alexander Potrezov, also at the meeting:

> Had we not felt such love (for Plekhanov), had we behaved toward him in a more circumspect manner, we would not have experienced such a

crashing comedown, such a spiritual cold shower. This was most severe, an injuriously severe, injuriously harsh lesson. Two young comrades "courted" an older comrade because of their great love for him, and, all of a sudden, he injects into this love an atmosphere of intrigue, and makes them feel—not like younger brothers—but like idiots who are being led around by the nose, like pawns that can be moved around with impunity, like ineffectual careerists who must be cowed and quashed.[25]

Lenin was able to arrange a compromise, a tactic that marked his victories until he assumed total power. The compromise involved a six-member editorial board; Plekhanov, Zasulich, Martov, Potrezov, Paul Axelrod, and Lenin all voted on issues. Plekhanov, however, was given two votes, which annoyed Lenin. The setup was difficult from the start because all six lived in different places. First, they had to decide where to print the paper. Plekhanov wanted Switzerland, presumably because he would have more control since he lived there, but Germany was chosen for its better printing facilities. Accordingly, Lenin settled in Munich, Germany, in early September.

Lenin's articles in *Iskra* appeared under his chosen revolutionary name and by which he was now becoming known. He did, however, use a vast number of pseudonyms throughout his life, such as Petrov or Frey, and even just initials, such as I, L, or V.Ul.

ALLIES VERSUS ENEMIES

In his Autopsy for an Empire: The Seven Leaders Who Built the Soviet Regime, *Dmitri Volkogonov explains Lenin's distinction between allies and enemies:*

"For Lenin, everyone was divided strictly into those who adopted a class (Leninist) position and were therefore allies, and those in the 'chauvinistical' camp who were therefore sworn enemies. Even in his article 'On the National Pride of the Great Russians', which every Soviet citizen was supposed to have read as a profoundly 'patriotic' piece of writing, Lenin asserted that 'the Great Russians should not "defend the fatherland" other than by wishing for the defeat of tsarism in any war, as the lesser evil for nine-tenths of Great Russia.' The slogans of pacifism [opposition to the war] and the idea of 'paralysing the war' were mocked by Lenin as 'ways of making fools of the working class', and he thought the notion of a 'democratic peace' without revolution 'profoundly wrong'."

THE MAN LENIN ADMIRED

Besides Karl Marx, Lenin probably admired no one more in his early years than revolutionary thinker Georgy Valentinovich Plekhanov, for many years the leading exponent of Marxism in Russia. Born in Gudalovka in 1856 to a family of minor nobility, Plekhanov attended the St. Petersburg Konstantinovskoe Military School fully intending to become an army officer. But during his second year at the Mining Institute, where he transferred, he suddenly abandoned his studies to throw himself fully into revolutionary activities.

Plekhanov became a leader of the organization Land and Freedom in 1877 and joined the underground movement. When the Russian Social Democratic Workers' Party (RSDWP) split into Bolsheviks and Mensheviks, Plekhanov initially sided with Lenin but spent most of his life trying to reunite the two factions.

During his last two decades, Plekhanov was intensely involved in literary and historical studies, to which he made significant contributions. He remained active in politics and supported the Allies during World War I because he believed that a German victory would be the end of the workers' movement in Russia. After the revolution in 1905, Plekhanov's influence over the revolutionaries began to decline, especially his involvement with Lenin. He supported the provisional government after the revolution of 1917, even though he was critical of many of its policies. He was rarely heard from after Lenin assumed power, and he died in Finland in 1918.

Lenin's aim was to create a unique publication to be circulated throughout Russia, which would in turn create a new social and political climate in this huge land. It was a formidable task because Russia was spread over great distances, and people in its European west and Asian east differed greatly. Its enormous peasant population, only newly emerged from serfdom, presented its own problems. Many peasants were illiterate and had little knowledge of government workings.

The first issue of *Iskra* was printed on December 24 (December 11 on the old Julian calendar). It urged readers to join the RSDWP against autocratic government and capitalist society.

WHAT IS TO BE DONE?

While busy with the publication of *Iskra*, Lenin sat down to write a short, extraordinary work during the winter of 1901 that gives shape to his doctrine. Using the title of Chernyshevsky's earlier work, *What Is To Be Done?*, Lenin laid out the principles that he would follow some sixteen years later. This was Lenin's blueprint in which his intentions are clear. According to Harold Shukman's book on the revolution, Lenin said, "If our little book *(What Is To Be Done?)* has not taught them social-democracy, then our revolution will."[26]

TO LONDON

Shortly after the publication in Germany of *What Is To Be Done?*, the printers of *Iskra* decided that printing the paper there was now too risky a venture because of antisocialist feelings. Another heated debate within the editorial board followed with Plekhanov again favoring Switzerland, but Lenin prevailed by arguing that a socialist press in England would be subject to less harassment than elsewhere on the continent.

Accordingly, Lenin and Krupskaya moved to London in March 1902, to oversee publication of the paper. Although at first dismayed by the hugeness of the city (the railroad station terrified Krupskaya), Lenin soon developed a genuine liking for the English capital during his stay there. Language was a problem at first. According to biographer Hill,

> at first they [Lenin and Krupskaya] could neither understand the spoken language nor make themselves understood. To teach themselves they went to meetings in Hyde Park (where they found the accent of an Irish atheist

easiest to follow), to churches, music-halls and pubs.[27]

Most of Lenin's days were spent at the British Museum in the Reading Room. It was the British Museum where Karl Marx, who lived in London from 1849 until his death in 1883, had done the research for *Das Kapital*. Lenin was able to get a ticket of admission to the Reading Room under the name of Jacob Richter. He generally spent afternoons meeting with other revolutionaries and attending to the business of the newspaper. Evenings were spent quietly at home with Krupskaya in their rented flat in Holford Square. In contrast to the picture of a violent, energetic revolutionary, as Lenin was described in later years, he was by temperament a quiet, modest man whose everyday activities varied little throughout his life.

Lenin also met Leon Trotsky for the first time in October 1902 in London. The twenty-three-year-old Trotsky, a brilliant writer, would later become a giant revolutionary in his own right and a close colleague of Lenin's. A number of other revolutionaries made their homes in the English capital during those years, including Martov and Zasulich who came over from Munich.

Lenin spent a year in London, his stay shortened by a vote of the editorial board to relocate the offices of *Iskra* to Geneva. His was the only dissenting voice, which again made him only too aware that he now disagreed with every other member of the board.

As Lenin encountered obstacles on his way to revolution, the stress often affected him physically. So when he and Krupskaya set off for Geneva in April 1903, Lenin was suffering from an excruciatingly painful attack of the shingles, a viral disease that attacked the nerve endings of his back and chest. In an effort to help, Krupskaya read a medical handbook and painted him with iodine, which did nothing to ease the pain of the condition.

THE SPLIT BEGINS

Lenin spent a couple of weeks recovering in Geneva. Thin and frail, he wore a long red beard and drooping mustache, bear-ing little resemblance to his later revolutionary portraits. But if he looked little like a revolutionary, he was about to begin the actions that would lead him down the desired path to total power.

The Second Congress of the RSDWP met on July 1903, in Brussels, Belgium. Soon after it opened, trouble began due to Lenin's desire for power. Lenin increasingly saw himself as the only one who could bring about a true Communist revolution in Russia. Said a biographer,

> Lenin's attitude was firm—he wanted power at all costs, and he was prepared to offer everything to every-

In London, Lenin spent much of his time at the British Museum (pictured) meeting other revolutionaries and managing his newspaper, Iskra.

Lenin meets with Russian peasants. To gain the support of the working classes, Lenin promised free education, freedom of worship, and the abolition of taxes.

body on condition that power was surrendered to him. To those who wanted a parliament he offered a parliament, to the proletariat he offered a dictatorship, to the peasants he offered the abolition of all taxes and freedom to work as they pleased, to the religious he offered freedom of worship, to parents he offered the free education of their children. This dazzling display of gifts, all put forward with the utmost seriousness, had the effect of sugar-coating the pill of a dictatorship. 'Yes, indeed, there will be a dictatorship,' Lenin seemed to be saying, 'but look how free everyone will be under it.'[28]

Lenin would offer anything if it achieved that purpose. Whether they were lies or Lenin truly believed what he was saying is unknown. The only thing that mattered to him was revolution. If it took a dictatorship to oust the tsar, that, too, was worth it so that the desired end at some point—the classless society of communism—would come true.

THE REAL BREAK

Soon after the Congress convened, some of the delegates were expelled from the country by the Brussels police, forcing a decision to reconvene in London on August 11.

COMRADE TROTSKY

A close and often troubling comrade to Lenin was Leon Trotsky, whose given name was Lev Davidovich Bronstein. He was born in Ukraine in 1879. Drawn into socialist circles at an early age, he was first arrested for revolutionary activity in 1898, spending nearly five years in prison in Siberia. While in exile he married and fathered two daughters. When he escaped from exile in 1902, his forged passport carried the name of Trotsky, which became his revolutionary pseudonym. Trotsky left his wife and family behind in Siberia, and the separation became permanent. He married again in Paris in 1903.

In 1905, Trotsky returned to Russia where he was involved in the St. Petersburg soviet and was consequently jailed in 1906, receiving a sentence of a second exile in Siberia. Once again he escaped, this time moving to Switzerland and then Paris at the outbreak of World War I.

After Trotsky joined Lenin for the revolution, he clearly became his first assistant during the civil war and war communism phase. He was Lenin's superior in administrative effectiveness, and some say his intellectual power, and did not hesitate to disagree with Lenin. However, Trotsky never managed the political maneuverings of Stalin and other comrades that would have put him firmly in the seat of power. After Lenin's death, Stalin emerged as the victor in the struggle for leadership. Stalin exiled Trotsky in 1929. Trotsky was assassinated by an agent of Stalin while in Mexico in 1940.

There, a split in the Congress broke open. This time the major disagreement was between Martov and Lenin. Although both men wanted a centralized party, Martov wanted a broad base open to anyone who supported the program. Lenin was insistent on a much smaller party, one open only to those active revolutionaries who were dedicated to the cause. A very real difference was taking shape here, but according to Shukman, the delegates stated it simply: "Lenin wants a narrow party, while Martov wants a broad one."[29] Martov was talking about a broad-based organization that would presumably incorporate the ideas of many. Lenin was talking about a highly disciplined, centralized party that would lead and guide many.

Lenin's central group would be hardened professionals who would lead the proletariat and all groups opposed to tsarism. That is the group he spoke of when he said, "Give us an organization of revolutionaries, and we will overturn Russia."[30] Martov and others disagreed with Lenin's view. They later declared that it was not a dictatorship of the proletariat (meaning one person acts as the leader although all members are equal) but a dictatorship over it (meaning one person whose will must be followed) and would eventually lead, as it did, to a one-man dictatorship.

During this major disagreement with Martov, Lenin acted as though he were on the edge of mental collapse. Rarely sleeping, eating little, ranting and raving at meetings, his brittle voice suggested that he was on the edge. Some might have thought he was on the edge of a mental breakdown, but even so, he was also on the edge of power.

The Congress voted between Martov and Lenin. Twenty-eight members supported Martov; twenty-three, including Plekhanov, supported Lenin. Over the next few days a frantic Lenin tried to think of ways to convince some of the delegates to change their minds. Then, when it seemed that he had lost, a disgruntled group of five Jewish Social Democrats simply walked out. Because they had originally voted for Martov, this produced a tie. Now Lenin shrewdly proposed that the Congress adopt *Iskra* as the

Lenin and Leon Trotsky (pictured) met in 1902, and the two were close comrades during the revolution.

party's sole newspaper instead of *The Workers' Cause*, which had been its main rival. Martov, not seeing a trap, agreed since he was closely involved with *Iskra*. As Lenin had hoped, two members who supported *The Workers' Cause* were angered over Martov's vote and left the Congress. Because they had originally supported Martov, Lenin now had a majority of two.

Lenin designated his group as the Bolsheviks (majority), and the opposing group led by Martov was known as the Mensheviks (minority). The Bolsheviks became dedicated to the RSDWP and would eventually be identified with the Russian Revolution. By manipulating the party members for his own cause, Lenin came into a position of power. For the time being anyway, no one would dispute him.

Although Lenin had won, his party's factions were barely speaking to one another. He managed to get three Mensheviks ousted from the editorial board of *Iskra*, leaving Martov as the sole representative. But when Plekhanov insisted on the return of the others to unite the party, Lenin handed in his resignation from the editorial board and central council of *Iskra*.

Although still a member of the RSDWP, Lenin was now on the outside of the party's power. In his article called "One Step Forward, Two Steps Back," he restated his belief in the necessity of a nar-

THE OPPOSITION

As Lenin's power grew, members of the RSDWP realized that he saw anyone who opposed his ideology as an emeny. Andrei Sinyavski explains Lenin's view in Soviet Civilization: A Cultural History:

"For Lenin, all opposition to bolshevism, to his power, or to his point of view was an expression of bourgeois class or political interests. As a marxist, Lenin did not recognize any individual ideology: everything was an expression of someone's class interests. Therefore, he lumped all his political opponents in the bourgeois camp which, he said, was bent on crushing the Bolshevik party and then Soviet power. Lenin salted all his articles and speeches with terms like 'agent of the bourgeoisie,' 'agents of international imperialism,' 'social traitors,' 'traitors to the working class,' and so on. A person's subjective honesty, his sense that he was neither bourgeois agent nor traitor, changed nothing in Lenin's view."

row party of professional revolutionaries. In an effort to regain Lenin's health, which had suffered greatly with mental strain and lack of sleep, over the next few months he and Krupskaya traveled in Europe.

In the fall of 1904, back in Geneva, Lenin announced publication of his newspaper *Vperyod* (*Forward*), which he said was the true organ of the working-class movement. Said Shukman, "Now his first concern was to carry on the struggle by means of 'the most varied and widespread agitation, by the spoken and written word.'"[31] As it turned out, for Lenin this was an appropriate time to launch a new antigovernment paper.

THE RUSSO-JAPANESE WAR

While Lenin was in Europe writing of coming revolution, other events in Russia motivated more supporters to join his cause. For some time a rivalry had existed between Russia and Japan over control in Korea and Manchuria. From February 8, 1904, to January 1905, Russia suffered nearly ninety thousand casualties in the Russo-Japanese War, and public discontent was widespread. The people began to complain about an army that could not win. The war led to food shortages and transportation breakdowns because so much money and effort were spent in fighting Japan. Once again, Russian workers faced starvation, and riots erupted.

While Lenin tried to build a political party to carry out his doctrine, one event, Bloody Sunday, brought his country closer to real revolution. That January 22

is often spoken of as the beginning of the Revolution of 1905, but it was not a revolution in the usual sense or as Lenin envisioned. Information reached Lenin in Europe about an outbreak of violence by the government, not by the oppressed.

THE MARCH ON THE WINTER PALACE

Bloody Sunday began—as do many tragic events—with peaceful intent. On that cold and biting winter day in the Russian capital, some two hundred thousand men, women, and children marched quietly through the streets carrying banners bearing the portrait of Tsar Nicholas II. Led by a former prison chaplain, Father George Gapon, the crowd was marching to the tsar's magnificent Winter Palace to present him with a document asking for a minimum wage and an eight-hour workday, among other governmental changes. There was no minimum wage at the time in Russia and workers' hours were determined by their employers. The people expected at the very least that the tsar would acknowledge their presence from a window in the Winter Palace.

Tsar Nicholas II, eldest son of Alexander, had been ruling the country since 1895. Autocratic and inept, he was ill suited for the complex tasks of leading such an enormous empire, especially one in a state of shifting attitudes and emotions. He had few intellectual pursuits and often regarded those who opposed him as malicious conspirators. It was this uncompromising viewpoint that helped to bring about Bloody Sunday and the overthrow of the House of Romanov.

Nicholas was not at the Winter Palace on the day of the march. As the huge crowd entered the square in front of the palace, someone in charge of the government troops, apparently frightened by the size of the approaching throng, panicked and ordered the soldiers to open fire. Within minutes, the snow was colored bright red as some one thousand Russian workers were killed or wounded on Bloody Sunday. No accurate number has ever been established. As it turned out, it was the tsar's uncle, Grand Duke Vladimir, who had given the order to fire, and in so doing he caused the fall of the House of Romanov.

Lenin heard about the massacre the next day in Geneva and was nearly frantic with excitement, concluding that at last the revolution had begun. However, it had not.

Chapter

5 The Aftermath of Bloody Sunday

The violence of Bloody Sunday triggered many small revolts in St. Petersburg and all over Russia and eventually led to greater discord and action. Bloody Sunday is important in Russian history because it altered the atmosphere in the country regarding revolution, it forced what could be seen as a drastic response from the tsar, and it dramatically changed how Lenin would spend the next years of his life.

The shootings that day so angered the Russian people that a general strike erupted in St. Petersburg and other cities. It was obvious to the tsar's advisers that the people had lost any faith they had held in the government. This caused the tsar, on his return to the capital, to take his advisers' recommendation to at least consider the creation of a legislative body, called the Duma.

Indeed, the first Duma convened on April 27. But it was soon obvious that this was a legislative body in name only, functioning at the whim of the tsar and without power. Four Dumas would be formed until the last was dissolved in 1917, but even though a small number of socialists took part, none of those participants held any power or influence in the government.

PREPARING TO RETURN

Meanwhile, Lenin was now flushed with the idea of revolution. Perhaps his tunnel vision toward this eventual outcome was best described by a Menshevik member of the RSDWP, who said, "There is no other man who is absorbed by the revolution twenty-four hours a day, who has no other thoughts but the thought of revolution, and who even when he sleeps, dreams of nothing but revolution."[32]

Lenin prepared to go to London for what he called the Third Congress of the RSDWP, which was a misnomer since only Bolsheviks attended. The Mensheviks held their own meeting in Geneva. Lenin was elected chairman of the all-Bolshevik Congress and was now the undisputed leader of the Bolsheviks.

Over the next two months in his socialist articles published for the Russian people, Lenin called for an armed uprising, urging them to obtain weapons, hold secret meetings, blow up police stations, and rob banks. He was convinced that the revolution could be successful by these methods, writing to party leaders in 1905, "I am absolutely horrified that people can go on talking about bombs for more than six months without making a single one."[33]

On June 16, the crew of the Russian navy cruiser *Potemkin*, tired of terrible food and worse living conditions, took the bold step of staging a mutiny while at target practice in the Black Sea at Odessa. They imprisoned or threw overboard all of the officers and tried to persuade other ships at anchor to join them in their fight for a better standard of living.

In an effort to take advantage of the mutiny, Lenin sent a comrade, Mikhail Vasilyev, to persuade all the ships at an-

THE BLOODY SUNDAY PRIEST

The man who headed the peaceful demonstration that led to what Lenin hoped would become revolution was a Ukranian priest named Father George Gapon (1870–1906). He had been sent to St. Petersburg where his duties brought him into contact with the city's workers. He felt that these people should ask for better working conditions. Like Lenin, Gapon was an effective speaker, lobbying for better conditions at the factories. Gapon felt the people owed their allegiance to both the church and the tsar. This changed on the morning of Bloody Sunday, when he led the huge crowd to the Winter Palace. After the bloody out-

come, Gapon went into hiding for a time and emerged as a rabid revolutionary who sought the forceful overthrow of the regime. He called the tsar the soul-murderer of the Russian empire. For these activities, Gapon was forced to flee the country when he received word that he would be executed by the tsar's police if caught.

Father Gapon and a large crowd of workers face the tsar's troops on Bloody Sunday.

chor there to join a revolution to take over the country. But the sailors were interested in their own livelihood, not Lenin's cause, and could not be persuaded.

However, events were heading toward revolution. Workers in St. Petersburg held elections in the city, forming what became known as *soviets*. A soviet is a council that performs both legislative and executive functions of government. Its use first appeared in 1905 when striking workers formed an organization that was dissolved by the tsar. In 1917, soviets sprang up all over Russia. They gained much of their authority in the people's eyes because they reflected the popular will.

The soviets tried to establish their own governments in defiance of the tsar. The Mensheviks of the RSDWP formed a government called the St. Petersburg Soviet of Workers' Deputies. Trotsky, now in Russia, was elected vice chairman and called for the people to stage a general strike. The citizens listened, and all railroad transportation stopped. Factories shut down. It was obvious that the Russian people were paying attention to this new organization. Soon the word *soviet* would become the alternative for the word *government*.

If the tsar did not yet grasp the seriousness of the situation, his advisers seemed to. Count Sergey Witte, a former minister of finance, gave clear warning to Nicholas of impending change when he said, "Russia has outgrown her existing structure. She is striving for a legal structure based on civil liberty."[34] He proposed that the tsar stop all repression of acts that did not threaten the state.

In response, Nicholas granted freedom of speech and the right to assemble to the Russian people. There was promise of a constitution. Witte was appointed prime minister. However, even with these concessions, Trotsky as head of the new soviet called for the strikes to go on.

This may have been revolution, but it was not the revolution Lenin had in mind, and he certainly was not leading it. He was compelled to return to Russia.

BACK ON RUSSIAN SOIL

Lenin returned to his homeland on November 21, 1905, uncertain of what lay ahead for his country and for himself. However, in October the tsar had issued a manifesto that promised civil rights, including no persecution of activists, so Lenin at least felt somewhat reassured that he would not be arrested on sight. Nonetheless, he and Krupskaya reached St. Petersburg via Germany, Sweden, and Finland and then lived underground, just in case the political situation tightened.

Lenin was busy for the next few weeks attending secret meetings in St. Petersburg and Finland. He had initially been surprised at how many people had joined in the general strikes. He opposed the Mensheviks' loose organization of revolutionaries and thought they should have been better prepared to further the cause of revolution once the strikes began. However, as he realized the power of the new soviet, he began to change his message. In his articles for *New Life*, he preached that the soviet of St. Petersburg

Abolishing the Church

Lenin's fund-raising schemes were often controversial. In a letter dated March 19, 1922, he declares that abolishing all churches will provide the Bolsheviks with needed funds:

"Now and only now, when people are being eaten in famine-stricken areas, and hundreds, if not thousands, of corpses lie on the roads, we can (and therefore must) pursue the removal of church property with the most frenzied and ruthless energy and not hesitate to put down the least oppositions.

We must pursue the removal of church property by any means necessary in order to secure for ourselves a fund of several hundred million gold rubles. . . . In order to get our hands on this fund of several hundred million gold rubles (and perhaps even several hundred billion) we must do whatever is necessary. But to do this successfully is possible only now."

simply was not encompassing enough; it should be organized to become the provisional revolutionary government of all Russia.

THE REVOLUTION DIES

Within a few months, it became clear that this was not the long-awaited revolution Lenin had envisioned. Perhaps mollified by the concessions of the tsar, the workers, especially in St. Petersburg, slowly became apathetic to new revolutionary demands by the soviets in St. Petersburg and other cities. Even when revolts, encouraged by the soviets, did take place, they were often poorly organized and quickly and ruthlessly crushed by the

tsar's police. The Black Hundreds, an organization backed by the empirical government, went on campaigns of terror throughout the country, killing thousands of citizens to discourage any further uprisings. When Trotsky called for a tax boycott in mid-December, the citizenry barely responded. However, when the tsar heard of the demand, all the members of the soviet executive committee were promptly arrested on his order. The tsar considered restoring his autocratic powers by rescinding rights to free speech and press. As he told one of his government officials, "It's their heads or ours. This situation can't last. I authorize you to take all measures that you consider necessary."[35]

In one last effort, the soviet called for a new general strike in late December. Although workers in St. Petersburg did not heed the call, an insurrection began in Moscow. Striking workers threw up barricades against the police, and for a time they held their own. But, finally, on December 31, the insurrection came to a brutal end when the tsar sent in the elite Semenevsky Guards and artillery from St. Petersburg. More than one thousand Moscovites, including eighty-six children, who were part of the demonstration or bystanders, were shot by the guards, blown apart by the artillery, or hacked to death by cavalry sabers. The Revolution of 1905 was over. In short order, the few civil liberties that had been granted were rescinded. Radical newspapers were suppressed, revolutionary leaders arrested.

Lenin was in Tampere (Tammerfors), Finland, when the revolution failed, attending a meeting of what was called the first All-Russian Bolshevik Conference. At the meeting, he met Joseph Stalin, a young Bolshevik delegate from the province of Georgia, for the first time. Many colleagues at the conference charged Lenin with moral responsibility for the tragic outcome in Moscow because he had long called for strikes and other disruptions. However, Lenin shrugged off the criticism, saying only that unfortunate occurrences were bound to happen in the march to revolution.

The following April, delegates met in Stockholm, Sweden, for the Fourth Congress of the RSDWP to elect members of the Duma, set to convene in May. Sixty-two Mensheviks and forty-two Bolsheviks attended. Lenin was urged by the Bolshevik side to keep party unity and peace for the sake of the next revolution. For instance, although both wings of the party voted against continuation of expropriations, such as bank robberies, to gain money for the revolution, Lenin spent much time at the conference in an argument for keeping them. However, Lenin finally did go along with the majority rule at the request of the Bolsheviks. Even though they were part of his party, Lenin regarded the Mensheviks as no less a hindrance to his future plans than the tsar.

When asked by a comrade what would happen in the future if the Bolsheviks remained a minority and had to submit to Menshevik authority, Lenin replied, "We won't permit the idea of unity to tie a noose around our necks, and we shall under no circumstances permit the Mensheviks to lead us by the rope."[36] Actually, Lenin had no intention of abiding by any rules of the Duma if they interfered with his own direction. The more Lenin ran into obstacles, the more he became determined to build the party and bring about the revolution in his own way. He would change Russia by himself if necessary into a Communist state. He would unite the workers, bring down the tsarist government, and set up a new country. More and more, in his mind, that new country could be brought into existence only by his will and only in his way.

The Retreat

Lenin returned to Russia and continued his writings and speeches that attacked the Duma, demanding action instead of words.

When military Bolshevik sympathizers gave Duma members a list demanding reforms, the tsar used it as an excuse to do away with the legislative body altogether. The Duma was dissolved in June 1907, with new elections to be held six months later.

With the Duma gone at least temporarily, Lenin felt he would be safer if he left the country. For some time he had been aware that his dreams of a true revolution were not yet ready to be realized. So he left Russia for Finland and then Geneva to regroup and lay plans.

The Fifth Congress of the RSDWP, with some 150 socialist groups attending from all over Russia and Europe, met in London in May 1907. This time Lenin and the Bolsheviks won control of the central committee. The following month Pyotr Arkadyevich Stolypin, the new prime minister, found an excuse to dissolve the second Duma. He had obtained a copy of a document in which the socialists urged the army to mutiny. Most of the RSDWP members in the second Duma were sent to labor camps by the tsar.

THE LONELY PERIOD

Now began what was probably the loneliest, most frustrating period of Lenin's life. The years until 1917 would sorely test his

Tsar Nicholas II opens the first Duma in May 1906. Lenin had no intention of following the Duma's rules if they conflicted with his goals.

strength, determination, and endurance. Fear for his safety had forced him to leave his country once more. His hopes for a revolution had failed. The tsar was back in control with all of his old autocratic powers. Those who had supported the revolutionaries returned to their former professional jobs. Even the workers, who were Lenin's hope for the revolution, seemed weary of the prolonged fight.

And within the RSDWP, Lenin faced opposition not only from the Mensheviks but from members of the Bolsheviks as well. Even his closest colleagues criticized him for placing revolution above party unity. Disagreements arose because Lenin was determined to see through his plans to raise money needed for revolutionary expenses any way that he could. One of his controversial schemes to raise money was the Tiflis affair. In June 1907, the Tiflis post office was expecting a large cash deposit from a state bank, delivered by stagecoach with armed soldiers—Cossacks—as escort. As the convoy proceeded through the main part of the city, bombs exploded in the streets. The Cossacks began firing, killing or wounding many innocent bystanders. The sacks of money mysteriously vanished. Months later, a number of Bolsheviks were arrested in Munich, Berlin, and Paris as they tried to exchange some of the stolen money. It was later learned that the money, as prearranged, went to Lenin to promote revolutionary activities. The

Joseph Stalin was the leader of the Tiflis holdup, a scheme of Lenin's to raise money for the revolution.

leader of the Tiflis holdup was known as Comrade Koba, whom the world would later know as Stalin.

Many Bolsheviks, who were not informed in advance of these activities, were angered. For Lenin, the outrage directed at him by his fellow party members meant little. He declared,

When I see social democrats proudly and smugly declaring "We are not anarchists, we're not thieves or robbers,

STEPA

So little is ever discussed about the personal side of Lenin that it is interesting to gain an insight into how he spent his minimal free time. Speaking of Lenin and Krupskaya, biographer Robert Service said in Lenin: A Biography:

"Like many childless couples, they made a fuss of their friends' children. In Krakow, they liked to entertain Stepan Zinoviev (or Stepa, as he was nicknamed) after Lenin had finished work for the day. The two of them ran about the house, clambering over furniture and crawling under beds. When Stepa's father or mother complained about the noise, Lenin would have none of it: 'Stop interfering: we're playing!' On another occasion he confided to the Zinovievs: 'Eh, it's a pity that we don't have such a Stepa.'"

we are above all that, we condemn partisan warfare," I ask myself if these people realize what they are saying.[37]

Despite Lenin's determination, this was obviously a lonely time for him. He wrote to his sister Maria from Geneva: "It's several days since we've landed in this hole, but we can't help ourselves. We will have to get used to it."[38] Lenin began to feel that he had reached a dead end in Geneva. He remarked to Krupskaya, "I feel as if I have come here to be buried."[39]

To keep busy while reforming his plans in Geneva, Lenin restarted *The Proletarian*, a Bolshevik underground newspaper that had been published for a period in 1905. Leon Trotsky, novelist Maksim Gorky, and other prominent Bolsheviks were asked to contribute articles.

Hoping that a change of scene would bolster his spirits, Lenin and Krupskaya moved to Paris to an apartment that they shared with her mother and his sister Maria. But a new environment did little. Lenin's health was poor and he suffered from sleeplessness. Lack of money was a constant problem. But most of his troubles stemmed from the fact that very little was happening in Russia at the time. There may have been much dissatisfaction within the country, but it was not bubbling to the surface as it had done earlier. It almost seemed as though the years of work up to this point had come to nothing. Enthusiasm for the socialists had declined to a mere trickle. They were ignored by the people and hounded by the police.

Yet, not even those dire circumstances would persuade Lenin that unity within the party was more important than an immediate call for revolution. At a congress of the Socialist International in Copenhagen in 1910, Lenin once again disagreed with the majority, this time over the matter of Russian trade unions. Prime minister Stolypin passed a law that made the unions legal as long as they stayed clear of politics. The Mensheviks applauded, but Lenin viewed the new law as a trap. He reasoned that, if they went along with Stolypin's tactics, the workers would never unite in a revolution and the RSDWP would come to an end.

THE SPLIT

Early in 1912, Lenin called for a small conference of his own Bolshevik supporters in Prague, then the capital of Bohemia. With none of the Mensheviks or others who disagreed with him attending, he persuaded the delegates to call the meeting the "Congress of the Russian Social Democratic Workers' Party." A law was then passed that declared the old central committee invalid, and a new one composed entirely by Lenin supporters was approved. With that trickery, the Bolsheviks became the controlling agent in the RSDWP.

Soon the Russian people became interested in revolution once again. In April, miners went on strike in Lena, Siberia, and their leaders were arrested. When the workers protested, the police shot hundreds of them, which resulted in more strikes all over the country. In one of the police raids on revolutionary headquarters in St. Petersburg, Stalin was arrested and sent into exile.

NOTHING BUT THE TRUTH

Founded in 1912 as an underground press by a staff composed of Lenin and two others, *Pravda*, which means "truth," is still published in Moscow. For the first six years of its publication, it was constantly suppressed by the tsar's forces but assumed its official role with the revolution of 1918. It remained the official organ of the Communist Party until 1991. Today, *Pravda* is distributed nationwide.

When operating as the newspaper of the Communist Party, *Pravda* sponsored and approved material that kept readers informed on Communist doctrine and theory. There was very little coverage of foreign news, except for domestic matters in foreign countries. In the pages of *Pravda*, Russian readers heard no sensational stories such as those that were published in Western newspapers. Its main purpose was to stress the official party line for its readers. Its editorials were often carried in other soviet papers, and Tass, the soviet news agency, sent them to other countries within the soviet bloc.

Lenin now began a daily labor newspaper in St. Petersburg called *Pravda* (*Truth*); today, it is still the major press in Russia. He used it to launch attacks against his opponents—mainly the Mensheviks—and the paper caught on with the industrial workers. After the first issue appeared on April 22, 1912, Lenin moved to Krakow, Poland. He feared that staying so far away in France would cause him to lose influence over the Bolsheviks in Russia, and if he returned to St. Petersburg, he would surely be arrested. Krakow was as close as he could get to Russia, and communications were good between the city and St. Petersburg. Lenin did regret staying out of Russia because he could not see his relatives, especially his mother who was ailing.

The split between the Bolsheviks and Mensheviks continued and was a topic of discussion at the International Socialist Bureau conference in July 1914. Lenin refused to attend but sent a representative who argued that party unity was simple to achieve: merely acknowledge Lenin's central committee as the committee of the entire party. The delegation refused. But a few days later, such infighting was forgotten as a great crisis suddenly engulfed all of Europe.

Chapter

6 War and Revolution

A chain of events beginning with the outbreak of World War I would hasten the tsar's downfall and open the door for Lenin's establishment of a new Russia. Following the assassination of Archduke Francis Ferdinand, heir to the Austro-Hungarian throne, on June 28, 1914, Austria declared war on Serbia. The war to end all wars, better known as World War I, had begun, with the Central Powers—Germany, Austria-Hungary, and Turkey—against the Allies—Great Britain, France, Russia, Italy, and Japan, to be joined by the United States in 1917.

A CALL FOR CIVIL WAR

Lenin's attitude toward World War I stunned even his own backers. Lenin wanted the imperialist war to be turned into civil war. He feared that an appeal to Russian patriotism would soften the people's attitude toward the present government. According to Richard Pipes,

> Throughout World War I Lenin rejected all manifestations of pacifism in the Russian and international socialist movements, insisting that the mission of socialists was not to stop

the war but to transform it into a civil conflict, that is, revolution.[40]

The real enemy, declared Lenin, was not the soldier in the opposite trench, but the autocratic government. He urged the people to turn guns on the rulers, not on each other. For Lenin, the true enemy was a system that had plunged them all into imperial terror. Therefore, they should destroy the system, not each other.

If Lenin was isolated before, he was even more so now. Most revolutionaries believed that all socialists should band together to ensure the defeat of the German military machine and then go about the business of revolution.

Lenin spent the war years in Switzerland where he continued to rage against any and all socialists who supported the war effort. He placed his hopes on Russia's quick defeat so he could once again focus the people's attention on revolution.

Indeed, for a time it did seem as though Lenin's wishes would be granted. Russia was ill prepared for war. Its soldiers were poorly trained and equipped and no match for the German military. Some 4 million Russians were killed or captured in the first year of the war. In the fall of 1914, Russia lost 170,000 men in a single battle at

Tannenberg in Germany. The tsar meanwhile was losing control of the country, leaning heavily on Rasputin, a mystic who had long influenced the tsar's wife, Alexandra. Rasputin advised Nicholas to take charge of the military himself, which he did. Meanwhile, the home front was falling apart. Wild inflation, severe food shortages, crippling strikes, and bitter despair against the royals from the military combined to cause chaos. Amidst the chaos, Rasputin was murdered in December 1916.

THE RUSSIAN REVOLUTION OF 1917

March 8, 1917, signaled the end of Russia as Lenin had known it and ushered in his long-sought dream of revolution. On that day a massive general strike took place in St. Petersburg, which was now called Petrograd. Four days later, the tsar's army began to defect and join the strikers. The Duma, already dissolved by the tsar, reorganized itself as the Provisional Committee of the Duma. Workers and soldiers then united to form the Petrograd Soviet of Workers' and Soldiers' Deputies to replace previous soviets in that city. Leaders of the Petrograd Soviet turned power over to a provisional government led by Mensheviks and socialist revolutionaries. Aleksandr Kerensky, son of Fyodor Kerensky who had written a letter of recommendation for Lenin back in 1887, was chosen as minister of justice for the provi-

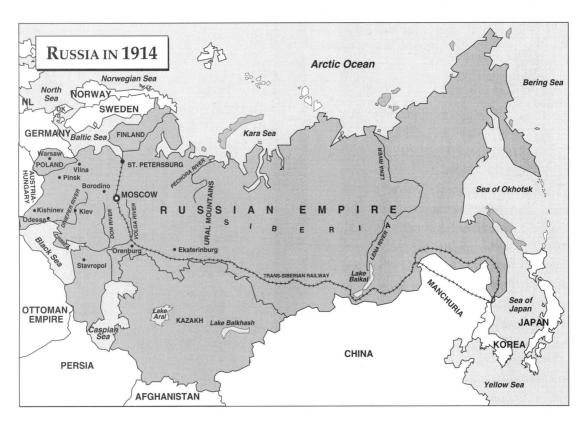

sional government. The first stage of revolution as Lenin had envisioned was under way.

On March 15, confronted with a new government and deteriorating conditions in his city, even the disengaged Nicholas realized that it was over. The tsar renounced the throne, in favor of his brother Mikhail, who refused the crown.

Lenin was nearly frantic once again being so far from the scene of the very events for which he had been working all his life. Early in April 1917, Lenin, Krupskaya, and close comrades left Zurich, Switzerland, and gained permission to travel through Germany in a sealed train, meaning it could make no stops through the country. They reached Sassnitz, a Baltic port, then ferried to Sweden where they rode another train through Finland to Russia. After long years of frustration and work, Lenin was going home—to his family, to his country, and to his revolution.

THE NEW DIRECTION

In the darkening hours of April 16, 1917, Vladimir Ulyanov, now known to all as Lenin, stepped from the train at Petrograd's Finland Station. He had been gone for a decade. Now forty-six years old, Lenin presented a round-shouldered, rather squat figure with piercing eyes that still caught the attention of all who looked into them. His worker's cap covered his bald head, making him blend into the crowd gathered at the station. To those who waited to hear him, Lenin greeted them in the name of the victorious revolution. Then he quickly spoke of a day not far off when the people would turn their weapons against capitalist exploiters.

In his study of the Bolshevik regime, Richard Pipes compares Lenin's ability to cast a spell over a crowd to that of leaders of Nazi Germany or Italian Fascism. He explained, "Lenin's method is to convince through compulsion. The hypnotist, the demagogue subordinates the will of the object to his own will . . . but the subject is convinced that he is acting out of his own free will."[41]

After the speech, the soldiers and sailors cheered and hoisted him to their shoulders, but Lenin's comrades thought he had gone quite mad because he had completely ignored those who spoke of unity in the cause of war defense. His speech indicated his intention to change the course of the revolution and, ultimately, Russian history. His fellow Bolsheviks believed in a two-stage revolution in which the government is taken over first by the bourgeois owners and then by the proletariat. Lenin had himself written time and again of a period that would pass before the proletariat took hold. Now, about one month after the bourgeoisie had gained control, he was declaring that the time for the takeover was today. Even more amazing, this man who now spoke to hundreds of citizens in St. Petersburg would in less than a year realize his dream and become the leader of the entire country.

Lenin also quickly made it clear that he gave no support whatsoever to the provisional government that had been set up. He believed that this government, led

Although Lenin had an unassuming appearance, his powers of persuasion were great. He was hugely successful in gaining support for a revolution.

by Mensheviks, would not push for the quick takeover that he urged. He wanted all Russians to refuse their support as well, labeling the government as imperialist and a leadership of capitalists. Only a soviet leadership, declared Lenin, a government directly ruled by workers, soldiers, and peasants, could fulfill the demands for peace and bring about the division of landed estate among the peasants. From this declaration came the oft-quoted battle cry of the revolution: "All power to the Soviets [councils]!" It was at this time that Lenin also proclaimed that since the Social Democrats had not truly supported the cause of the workers, the Bolsheviks should distinguish themselves and their revolution by renaming themselves as Communists.

A TIME OF PERSUASION

For the next several months, Lenin spent his time writing pamphlets and making speeches to persuade his fellow Bolsheviks that now was the time for revolution. Before beginning his work, however, he made a trip to the grave of his mother, who had died the previous July at the age of eighty-one. Always deeply attached to his mother, Lenin was greatly saddened by her death and the fact that he was out of the country when she died.

This was the period in Russian history that Lenin referred to as "dual power." Instead of assuming power, the Petrograd Soviet had turned it over to the provisional government. Now, declared Lenin, the Bolsheviks must persuade workers, soldiers, and peasants that state power must be taken back from that body. Once a soviet government was established, negotiations must begin to stop the war at once, calling for a general peace on all fronts. Kerensky, as head of the provisional government, was determined that Russia must win the war.

The task before Lenin was great. Not only were the Bolsheviks still in the minority in the country, but most of them did not even agree with Lenin's philosophy of an immediate takeover. The country itself was unstable. The abdication of the tsar had left Russians with a sense of freedom, but it was freedom with bewilderment about their lives and their futures. The strain of three years of terrible suffering and devastation from the war had left its mark. A general lawlessness seized the land.

Lenin was undaunted by the task before him and single-minded in his determination to bring first the Bolsheviks and then the rest of the country to his view. Indeed, Lenin was a forceful persuader. Within about a month of his arrival in Petrograd, he had convinced the Bolshevik Party Central Committee to endorse his program: withhold power from the existing provisional government and establish a government that would follow his leadership. From that would come peace negotiations for the war and then all landlords' estates

Lenin addresses a crowd. Lenin made many speeches to convince the Bolsheviks that the time for revolution had come.

would be confiscated (without payment to the owners) and all land would be nationalized and divided among the peasants. Following that, the government would tightly control privately owned industry for the benefit of the workers.

A Change in Fortunes

By June, escalating events seemed to favor Lenin. An essential part of his drive for power was the return to Russia of Leon Trotsky. He had been in exile in the United States publishing a socialist newspaper in Brooklyn, New York. Trotsky and Lenin had severely disagreed through the years, but Trotsky sensed that only Lenin had the strength and determination to win in this struggle. In addition, Trotsky, like Lenin, believed in a worldwide revolution in which socialists would take over every country. Trotsky was also a most effective public speaker, and his previously independent followers, known as the United Social Democrats, now sided with the Bolsheviks.

In late June, Kerensky ordered a major military offensive against the Germans, under pressure from Britain, France, and the United States, which had now joined the war effort. Successful at first, the campaign soon failed and the Germans counterattacked. Army morale, already disastrously low, fell to a new depth, and hundreds of thousands of Russian troops deserted.

On July 1, 1917, many socialists organized a mass rally to indicate the people's support for the provisional government. Instead, the provisional government was quite horrified to see that the vast majority of demonstrators carried signs supporting the Bolsheviks. It seemed obvious that the people were growing weary of Kerensky's leadership and more favorable toward Lenin's ideas.

On July 16, Lenin returned to Petrograd from Finland where he had been taking a short rest. Hundreds of thousands of demonstrators had gathered in the city demanding that the provisional government relinquish power and turn it over to the soviet. Word spread that some twenty thousand sailors based at Kronstadt in the Gulf of Finland were on their way to join the demonstrators. Lenin was again convinced that the revolution had begun. Instead, Kerensky called in troops who were loyal to the government and demanded the arrest of Lenin and other Bolshevik leaders. Lenin was accused by Kerensky of being an agent for the Germans.

Lenin managed to escape capture and returned to Finland where for the next three months he worked on his pamphlet, *State and Revolution*. Although never completed, it is Lenin's doctrine of power. In it, he speaks of a new state. He said that the proletarian revolution must do away with government as it now existed and introduce direct rule by workers and peasants in order to achieve a classless, stateless Communist society.

With Lenin in hiding once again, Kerensky seemed more secure in his hold on the provisional government. He even moved into the tsar's Winter Palace, after sending Nicholas and his

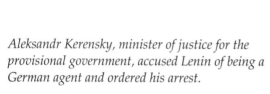

Aleksandr Kerensky, minister of justice for the provisional government, accused Lenin of being a German agent and ordered his arrest.

family into exile in a small town in Siberia. In the meantime, the war was draining the country's resources and the economy was in a severe downfall. Kerensky, despite his almost dictatorial powers, seemed incapable of stopping the slide. Lenin was kept aware of all activities with the help of Stalin and other close comrades. Stalin slipped out of Petrograd with ease to visit Lenin, who was disguised as a peasant and lived in the barn of a Finnish family.

THE REVOLUTION AT LAST

Until September 1917, the Bolsheviks had remained a minority in all soviet organizations in the country. However, with increasing support from workers, soldiers,

and peasants, a Bolshevik majority was now voted in the Petrograd Soviet, where Trotsky had become chairman, and other soviets as well. For Lenin, the time had come for his return.

Lenin returned to Petrograd in October, putting himself at considerable risk of capture by Kerensky's government. Kerensky was aware of Lenin's intentions to oust him and had issued another warrant for his arrest. Lenin went into hiding for a few days and then called a meeting of the Bolshevik central committee on October 23. It took a heated debate, but with Trotsky's support he convinced the members to prepare for an armed takeover. Plans were made immediately to enlist the support of the military and also to ready the Bolshevik workers' militia, known as Red Guards.

IMPECCABLE TIMING

In this excerpt from Autopsy for an Empire: The Seven Leaders Who Built the Soviet Regime, *author Dmitri Volkogonov points out the impeccable timing of Lenin's takeover on November 7, 1917.*

"Lenin was able to determine the precise moment at which the government was totally paralysed and defenceless, when if the Bolsheviks did not seize the moment, others would. The American journalist John Reed, who became a hero of the revolution, recorded Lenin saying on 3 November: '6 November will be too soon to act; the eighth too late. We have to act on the seventh, the day the [Second] Congress [of Soviets] opens.'"

Still the central committee delayed, fearful of taking the actual final step. Lenin, worried that the time would pass for a successful insurrection, pressed for a date to be named. On the evening of November 6, he sent a letter to central committee members exhorting them to act and declaring that any more delay might be fatal to the cause of revolution.

On the morning of November 7, 1917, the long-held dream of Lenin was realized. The Petrograd Soviet began the revolution that would forever change the country of Russia and the history of the world. Meeting only slight resistance, the Red Guards and soldiers and sailors overthrew the provisional government. Two days later the revolutionaries took the former government strongholds and secured the power stations. Finally, the revolutionaries took the Winter Palace, although

Kerensky and his men managed to escape in cars sent over from the British and American embassies.

Only then did Lenin come out of hiding. He had spent most of his forty-seven years building a party, and now that party was in control of one of the largest countries in the world. As a biographer said, "For him the main thing was to create the institution of control."[42] Lenin felt that Russians were now ready for a leader to manage that power.

Lenin issued a manifesto "To the Citizens of Russia." He wrote,

> The Provisional Government has been deposed. State power has passed into the hands of the organ of the Petrograd Soviet of Workers' and Soldiers' Deputies, the Revolutionary Military Committee, which heads the Petrograd proletariat and the garrison.

The cause for which the people have fought—namely, the immediate offer of a democratic peace, the abolition of landed proprietorship [ownership], workers' control over production, and the establishment of Soviet power—this cause has been secured.

Long live the revolution of workers, soldiers and peasants![43]

That evening Lenin spoke to an assembled congress of soviets. He announced a call for immediate peace with all nations involved in World War I and a three-month armistice with Germany. He also declared that private property no longer existed and all land belonged to the state.

SAVING THE REVOLUTION

Starting a revolution is one thing; sustaining it is another. Lenin may have seized the country, but it was a precarious hold. The Mensheviks were certainly not pleased with the takeover by Lenin. They preferred that Kerensky return to power. Kerensky did actually attempt a comeback with a few hundred Cossacks, but Lenin easily overcame them, although no blood was shed. Kerensky escaped once again and eventually emigrated to the United States.

Lenin's first order of business was to name a government. Trotsky suggested

the term "commissar" be used for leadership positions instead of "minister" because the latter was a word used to indicate positions of power in the tsarist regime. Trotsky became commissar of foreign affairs, and Stalin was assigned as commissar of nationalities. A Council of People's Commissars, a fifteen-member, all-Bolshevik executive body, became the first soviet government, and since it elected Lenin as its chairman, he became the head of state.

Lenin was well aware that his hold on the country was shaky at this point. He

Lenin stands atop a tank during the revolution of 1917. The revolutionaries easily overthrew the provisional government.

had taken actual control with relative ease, but not all Russians agreed with him and his ideas. Much of the military was anti-Bolshevik. The country was huge, deteriorating, and seemingly unmanageable. Lenin knew that he had to establish control quickly and firmly and he would keep control by whatever measures possible. These included closing all publishing houses and newspapers not controlled by the Bolsheviks in order to keep only one party line before the people. Lenin established the All-Russian Extraordinary Commission for Combating Counterrevolution and Sabotage in December. This secret police force, known as Cheka, was ruthless in its hunting down of enemies of the revolution. Thus began Lenin's campaign of terror, which he believed was necessary and justified to obtain his political ends. The Cheka quickly established tactics as brutal and oppressive as the tsar's had been. It answered only to the executive committee and to Lenin.

Before the revolution, Lenin had promised that elections would be held for a democratic assembly. It would in turn draft a constitution, a long-held dream of many Russian revolutionaries. Although Lenin feared that the Bolsheviks might not be strong enough to win a popular election, he felt that he had to honor his promise.

FREEDOM OF RELIGION?

Following the Russian Revolution, Lenin established powerful sanctions against churches. While many Russians felt that Lenin's policies were oppressive, writer Aldo Quinto Lazzari believed the laws allowed a freedom of religion that the country had not experienced under tsarist rule. In his book, How I "Discovered" Religion in Russia, *Lazzari writes,*

"The Declaration of Rights of the Peoples of Russia, adopted by the Soviet Government, headed by Lenin, immediately after the triumph of the October Revolution, abolished all national and religious privileges and restrictions and the division of religions into 'dominant,' 'tolerable,' and 'intolerable' ones. . . . In 1902 [Lenin] formulated the principle of separation of the church from the state and the school from the church. This programme was adopted in 1903. Lenin emphasized the need to fight for . . . the right of every person to adhere to any faith or to change faith. 'There should be no established religion or church,' he wrote. 'All religions and all churches should have equal status in law.'"

LENIN MAKES PEACE

Radical German theologian Carl Friedrich Bahrdt endured censorship and criticism from church officials for expressing enlightened views such as the following, quoted in What Is Enlightenment? *edited by James Smith.*

"Lenin was prepared to make peace with the Central Powers [Germany] on any terms as long as they left him a power base. The resistance which he encountered in party ranks grew out of the belief (which he shared) that the Bolshevik government could survive only if a revolution broke out in Western Europe and the conviction (which he did not fully share) that this was bound to happen at any moment.

Lenin's primary concern was for the immediate survival of his government. Lenin argued that "Our tactics ought to rest . . . [on the principle of] how to ensure more reliably and hopefully for the socialist revolution the possibility of consolidating itself or even surviving *in one country* until such time as other countries join in."

So, he allowed the election to take place—the country's first free election and its only one for many decades to come. The Bolsheviks were badly defeated. Ironically, Lenin reacted just as the tsar had and simply dissolved the assembly. The opposition, although it had defeated the Bolsheviks, was not united enough to revolt. Russia was now a one-party country with Lenin as its head.

THE PEACE TREATY

Lenin knew that his suffering country needed peace immediately if it (and his government) were to survive. That meant negotiating a peace treaty with the Germans before they decided to invade Russia. However, the Allies refused to help Russia withdraw from the war and would not deal with the new soviet government. Therefore, Lenin decided to enter peace negotiations alone, even though Trotsky cautioned a delay, feeling that a revolution was about to erupt in Germany.

Lenin sent Trotsky to the peace conference with the Central Powers at the German-occupied Polish town of Brest-Litovsk in December 1917. Germany already occupied Russian territory including a large part of agriculturally rich Ukraine. At the peace table, Germany demanded even more land and a considerable amount of gold rubles. Lenin declared in opposition to his government's other leaders that there was no choice but to accept the treaty on Germany's terms. He knew he would lose his hold on the country if peace were not negotiated immediately. He announced that if Russia did not sign the peace treaty, he would resign from the government. Believing they were not strong enough to lead the country, the other leaders went along with Lenin's demand. Above all, Lenin sensed that the Russian people were utterly weary of war.

The Treaty of Brest-Litovsk was signed in March 1918, under terms humiliating to Russia. It lost one-fourth of its land, including Poland, Ukraine, and the Baltic States, and about one-third of its population. But Russia's involvement in World War I had ended. According to *The Histo-rian*, "Thus, in early 1918, when Lenin advocated terror against perceived enemies of the state, it seemed a minor cruelty amidst the continuing battles of the war."[44]

Lenin accepted the terms of the treaty because he truly had convinced himself that an international socialist revolution might well follow, in which case the German monarchy would be destroyed and Russia would regain its territory. Indeed, when the Allies were victorious several months later, Germany was forced to give up the territories taken in the peace treaty Lenin had signed. In the interim, the treaty had bought him time to put his country together.

Chapter

7 The All-Powerful Revolutionary

Once in power, Lenin was determined to bring communism to Russia and to the world, no matter what the cost. An article on the extraordinary tasks Lenin faced during this period states,

> The idea of a commune-state, . . . without bureaucracy and without privileged people, still seemed achievable to Lenin during the period of the Brest peace. . . . Lenin's starting point was that only a strong central authority was capable of guaranteeing the restoration of the economic links which had been destroyed by revolution and war. It alone could repair organised contacts with the countryside, normalise the financial system and introduce order and discipline.[45]

CIVIL WAR

The obstacles facing the new soviet government would surely have seemed insurmountable to anyone with less drive and determination than Lenin. Damage from the war and food shortages crippled the cities. The entire Russian railway system had fallen to its lowest operating capacity. Peasants were confronted with falling currency values and few goods to buy even if they did have money. So, the peasants reasoned it was not worth their backbreaking work to plant any more crops than they needed to feed themselves. Unemployed workers starved in the cities where factory after factory closed due to the failing economy. It is estimated that some 7 million Russians died of starvation from 1918 to 1920.

To add to these pressures, in the spring of 1918 Lenin's government faced civil war from the so-called White armies, meaning all those against the revolution. The soviets had long been known as "Reds," the color having become the symbol of communism. These councils adopted a red flag after the banner of the French Revolution. Anticipating civil war well before its onset, Lenin had moved the Russian capital from Petrograd to Moscow shortly after signing the peace treaty with Germany. He felt that the old capital was too exposed to attack from either the Germans or the Whites. The move was not popular, especially with the workers in Petrograd who felt abandoned. In fact, Lenin and his government leaders had to get out of town under cover of darkness.

Once in Moscow, which remains Russia's capital city, Lenin moved into the Kremlin. It was originally a fortress built in 1156 and had been the seat of power for generations of tsarist rulers. Lenin and Krupskaya moved into a five-room, sparsely decorated apartment in another building of the Kremlin because Lenin did not want to be associated with the affluence of the former empire.

The White Army that faced the Reds was formed mainly from the remnants of the tsar's forces. They were led by former generals and admirals who fought desperately to overthrow the soviet regime. In addition, they were assisted by the Allies, who were angered by Lenin's decision to negotiate peace with Germany and refused to recognize the soviet government.

Besides the money and weapons given to the Whites, the Allies sent in about fifty thousand Allied troops, including Americans, to help stop the revolution.

Only inspired leadership from Lenin managed to save the soviet regime and the Russian Socialist Federative Soviet Republic (RSFSR) as the country was now known. He was like a man possessed, working nineteen-hour days from his office in the Kremlin, barking out orders, directing campaigns against the White forces. Even in the crumbling and disorganized economy, he managed to find resources to keep the Red Army fighting under Trotsky's command.

It was Lenin's uncanny political leadership that saved his government. By cleverly proclaiming that all people had the

Once in power, Lenin moved into the Kremlin in Moscow. The Kremlin remains the seat of power in Russia today.

right, no matter what their ethnic background, to determine their own government—something the Whites did not say—Lenin won the sympathy of all non-Russian groups within the country. This allowed Russia to remain a more or less unified multinational state. Then he declared the proletariat, the workers, would be first in line for food, housing, and political power, so he won their favor too. He told the peasants they could take all the land from the crown, church, and nobility without compensation paid. Naturally, the peasants sided with Lenin.

THE DEATH OF THE TSAR

Lenin also made another, more tragic political choice during this period of civil war. It points out his will to exact any consequences if it furthered his drive to complete socialism. After the tsar's abdication, Nicholas and his family had been exiled to a small town in Siberia. However, in May 1918, Lenin had them moved to Ekaterinburg (now Sverdlovsk), a Bolshevik stronghold on the eastern slopes of the Ural Mountains, where it was reported that Lenin himself planned to go if the Whites overran the country. He took this step because he was afraid that Siberia was too easy for White forces to reach the tsar. The Red Guards kept watch over the royals, who were allowed no communication with the outside world. Lenin greatly feared the possibility of Nicholas being returned to the throne.

At first, Lenin debated whether to put the tsar on public trial. However, he de-cided to punish him with death. One biographer explained the decision in this way:

> The verdict was death for Nicholas and his family and the destruction of the bodies "in order not to give the counter-revolutionaries an opportunity of using the bones of the Czar to play on the ignorance and superstition of the masses." A special commission was appointed to carry out this order. [Therefore, on July 17, 1918,] it was decided to bring the entire family into the [family's] cellar and there carry out the sentence. Until the very last moment the Romanovs were unaware that they were to be executed. At midnight they were awakened, ordered to dress, and go down to the cellar. In order not to arouse their suspicions, they were told that a "White" attack upon the house was expected that night. All the other inmates of the house were ordered to assemble in the cellar as well. When they had all congregated, the verdict was read to them and all eleven members of the Romanov family, Nicholas, his wife, his son Alexei, his four daughters, and the members of his suite were shot on the spot.[46]

The bodies were taken a few miles away and burned. However, the government released only the news that the tsar had been executed. In fact, to ward off any sympathy for the executions, an official announcement said, "The rest of the family had been evacuated to a safe place."[47] Because of that and because there were no

Fearful that Nicholas II would regain the throne, Lenin ordered the execution of the tsar, his wife, Alexandra, their children, and members of their household.

remains, legends persist that members of the Romanov family escaped to the West. Shortly after the execution, other members of the Romanovs were also executed in the Urals, and Grand Duke Mikhail, the tsar's brother, was shot by the Cheka in the city of Perm. Violence against all potential enemies was now the order of the day.

THE RED REIGN OF TERROR

After the Brest-Litovsk peace, Lenin escalated his terrorist polices. He used the Cheka and concentration camps to punish anyone he felt was an enemy of the state. He sent members of his party to "remove" unwanted people. Lenin felt that terror was a necessary means for establishing complete rule. Years earlier in Geneva, he had explained his theory of what revolutionists must do when they come to power and face someone from the old regime. Lenin said,

> We'll ask the man, "where do you stand on the question of the Revolution? Are you for it or against it?" If he is against it, we'll stand him up against the wall. If he is for it, we'll welcome him into our midst to work with us.

To which Krupskaya had replied, "Yes, and you'll shoot precisely those that are better men for having the courage to express their views."[48]

Lenin knew that one of the ways in which he could use terror for control was

THE LEGEND LIVES

When Tsar Nicholas II and his wife Alexandra were shot to death in Ekaterinburg on July 17, 1918, their son Alexei and four daughters, Olga, Tatiana, Maria, and Anastasia, died with them—or so it is believed. However, after the assassination ordered by Lenin, there were several reports that Anastasia survived. She was the youngest of the tsar's daughters, born on June 5, 1901, which would have made her seventeen years old at the time of the killings. Because the bodily remains of the victims were never found, the legend lives on.

Not long after the executions, several women from outside of Russia claimed to be Anastasia, and each said she had somehow escaped the shooting and the country. It is believed that these women sought the fame and prestige that comes with being the survivor of the royal family. Thus began the legend. The most famous of these reports came from a woman known as Anna Anderson; critics said she was really a Polish woman named Franziska Schanzkowski. Through the last decade of her life, she had tried to win recognition as the legal heir to the Romanov fortune but was rejected by the German courts.

According to legend, Anastasia (third from left) survived the execution of her family.

through the Cheka, the soviet's most ruthless police organization. Its leadership was given to a Polish-born veteran and a Bolshevik named Feliks Edmundovich Dzerzhinski. From a wealthy landowning family, he was in jail in Moscow for political activities when the revolution began. He defended Lenin's philosophy of using

Feliks Dzerzhinski, leader of the Cheka, agreed with Lenin that all enemies of the revolution had to be eliminated.

any means to the desired revolution's end in a speech to the press when he said,

> We exist on a basis of organized terror, which is an absolutely essential element in revolution. We counter the enemies of the Soviet Government with terror and extirpate the criminals on the spot. . . . And just as the Red Army in the civil war cannot stop to see whether it is wronging individuals, and is obliged to pursue a single aim, i.e., the victory of the revolution over the bourgeoisie in the same way the Cheka is obliged to defend the Revolution and crush the enemy, even if its sword sometimes chances to strike the heads of innocent people.[49]

Dzerzhinski, like Lenin, understood that until all the enemies of the revolution were crushed and all would-be enemies banished or made too afraid to act, Lenin would never be in full power.

In later years, the organization known as Cheka assumed different acronyms, such as OGPU, NKVD, and MVDZ, but its mission remained the same. It is estimated that by 1922, the Cheka, with the knowledge and consent of Lenin, had accounted for some 240,000 deaths while stamping out soviet political enemies. People might be arrested or killed if their race, religion, political beliefs, and countless other actions could somehow be construed as harming the state.

THE ASSASSINATION ATTEMPT

Because he endorsed the use of terror organizations such as the Cheka, Lenin was

Lenin is shot in an assassination attempt. He survived and returned to work two weeks later.

well aware that attempts on his own life were a very real possibility. The Cheka was ordered to show its full strength on August 30, 1918. On that day Lenin gave two speeches in Moscow and was picked up by his regular chauffeur, S.K. Gil. After the second speech at the Mikhelson Armaments Factory, he waved good-bye to the crowd and walked to his car. Before he reached it, three shots were fired. As one biographer described,

> Lenin had fallen to the ground. He had been hit twice on the left side of his body. One bullet lodged in his neck, the other in the lower part of his shoulder. Bleeding profusely, he was bundled into the vehicle by Gil and others. The car sped away from the scene of the shooting to the Kremlin.[50]

Lenin was taken to his apartment because the Kremlin at the time had no hospital or clinic or even a doctor, although doctors were quickly summoned. The rumor spread that he had died, although it was soon evident that he would recover and actually returned to work within two weeks. However, he had narrowly escaped death.

The would-be assassin was said to be Fanya Kaplan, who had approached Lenin as he walked to the car. Gil claimed to have identified her, but later reports show it is doubtful he could have seen clearly since he was inside the car at the time. She denied being the shooter. Many said Kaplan made an unlikely assassin because she had been blinded in 1912 during some activist bombings and had only partially recovered her sight. According to biographer Robert Service,

> It is well within the bounds of possibility that a group of Socialist Revolutionaries, working independently of their Central Committee, had engineered the assassination attempt. It is also plausible that Kaplan belonged to them. . . . Yet if she was at the Mikhelson Factory as the member of such a group, the others would surely not have chosen her as the assassin. . . . Kaplan was to be adjudged guilty. There would be no trial, only an announcement that the death sentence had been carried out.[51]

However, many other of Lenin's biographers do believe that Kaplan was the attempted assassin. She was sentenced to death shortly after the shooting but mysteriously was shot to death in prison on September 3.

THE NEW ECONOMIC POLICY

Before the civil war, the Bolsheviks, who now called themselves the Russian Communist Party, began a program under Lenin's direction known as "war communism." Its aims were basically to eliminate free enterprise in the country and to establish state control of the entire economy. These had been Lenin's aims all along; the war made a convenient excuse. During the civil war, practices were set up such as extending the workday, relocating workers without their approval to locations where the government felt they were needed, and exacting heavy fines for absence from work. The government began to eliminate competition in industries and set fixed prices for goods.

The civil war between Reds and Whites was over by the end of 1920. The Whites, although they achieved many victories, lacked a united political policy, a fact that soon began to discourage their Allied backers. Lenin's government was still standing, but the devastation of the country, with civil war heaped upon world war, was staggering. Some 8 million Russians died during the civil war years, the vast majority from starvation. Something had to be done quickly.

At the beginning of the war, as part of war communism, Lenin had started a policy toward the peasants that now threatened the economy. Desperate for food to sustain the Red Army in fighting the Whites but lacking money to pay for it, Lenin ordered the taking of surplus grain from the peasants without compensation. As Pipes noted in his work on the revolution, war communism was a term "coined to justify the disastrous consequences of economic experimentation by the alleged [demand] of the Civil War and foreign intervention. . . . These experiments left Russia's economy in shambles."[52]

Naturally, the peasants resisted the policy at first. However, when the White troops overran parts of the country, they took back the land and restored it to the former owners, punishing the peasants who had taken it in the first place. This kept most of the peasants on the side of the government despite Lenin's grain policy.

When the civil war ended, the peasants refused to give up any more grain without payment and threatened to revolt. Lenin had little choice but to give in. In March 1921, he instituted a New Economic Policy (NEP). It put an end to war communism, and it allowed the peasants to sell their grain on the open market. Capitalism had partially returned to Russia. Lenin realized that his action was a retreat from communism, yet he would tolerate even that if he felt it meant the survival of his revolution. The effects of the NEP on the Russian economy were quick and beneficial.

THE PLACE OF COMMUNISM

Lenin may have allowed a retreat to capitalism when it came to selling grain on the open market, but he would tolerate no retreat when it came to politics. With food supplies still dangerously low and grievances high throughout the country, the general unrest continued to threaten soviet rule. In March 1921, just before the NEP came into effect, a group of sailors at Kronstadt naval base, most of them sons

Peasants strongly resisted Lenin's seizure of their grain without compensation during the war. When the war ended, Lenin allowed peasants to sell their grain on the open market.

THE KRONSTADT REBELLION

When sailors at the Kronstadt naval base rebelled in 1921, Lenin believed that, to stay in power, he would have to slaughter tens of thousands of them. Biographer Robert Payne sums up the episode in The Life and Death of Lenin.

"The sailors of Kronstadt were brave men, but inept revolutionaries. They believed wholeheartedly in their pacific propaganda. It was as though they suffered from some strange disease compounded of hope and benevolence, and believed they could infect the whole of Russia with their disease. It never occurred to them until too late that Lenin was implacable and ruthless, and would sign the death warrant of the Kronstadt sailors with the same careless ease as he had signed the death warrant of the bourgeoisie."

of peasants, began a revolt. Among other things, they demanded freedom of speech. Lenin sent in the Red Army and Cheka. The sailors at Kronstadt were quickly wiped out.

From the moment Lenin established soviet rule in Russia and stepped into the seat of power, he had two aims regarding international relations. First, he had to crush a united front against soviet Russia. With the end of the civil war and of Allied intervention, that aim was largely accomplished. Then he dreamed of stimulating proletarian revolutions all over the world.

That was Lenin's hope when he had founded the Third, or Communist, International in 1919. It was a call for revolutionaries everywhere to follow the example of the Russian Bolsheviks. If revolutions were successful elsewhere, Russia could break out of its isolation of being surrounded by capitalists.

At the Third International, Lenin held up the Russian Communist Party as a model for all would-be revolutionists. He had been successful where others had failed. However, despite Lenin's genius for persuasion, his dream of a world republic of soviets never materialized, although his call for people's rights carried a promising message. All this effort may not have stimulated the results Lenin wanted, but Russia's success as a model for communism and the world's perception of Lenin as a strong leader kept away those who might have wanted to topple his government. And it did give the Russian Communists the sense that they were not the only ones fighting for the cause of revolution.

Lenin would not be deterred from his expressed goal of world communism, no matter how unrealistic. An article in *The New Republic* made that point:

Lenin's accomplishments will probably go down in history with those of Alexander, Caesar and Napoleon, but even this paragon of tough-mindedness could fall prisoner to ideological dreams and political hopes. He did deceive himself on a few big matters. His dogged insistence that the West, including England, was on the verge of revolution makes a reader wonder what was in his head.[53]

By 1921, peace had come to Russia, and Lenin's Communist Party had defeated its obvious enemies. Yet Lenin was aware that the peasants and a large portion of Russian workers were disenchanted with the revolution and its promises. For one thing, except for the NEP, no power had been returned to the people. The ruthless slaughtering of the Kronstadt sailors—the last real revolt of the Russian people—dashed the hopes of many Russians who had felt that the revolution would bring in a democratic society. Some of them, including Maksim Gorky, well-known Russian novelist who joined the Bolsheviks in 1903, left the country. He would not return for nearly a decade, long after Lenin's death.

Lenin's reaction to those who opposed him was to install tighter controls both within and without the party. There would be no opposition. Anyone who opposed the rule of the Bolsheviks would be dealt with in the harshest terms, including death. In this way, Lenin, who had intellectually always spoken against dictatorship, became himself the dictator of Russia.

8 The Last Years

Lenin never worked with more determination than he did during the last two years of his life, when he tried to resolve the corruption of his socialist ideals. At the Tenth Congress held in Petrograd in March 1921, while the Red Army was marching across the frozen Gulf of Finland to strike down the Kronstadt rebellion, Lenin was outlining his economic policy and calling for a ban on all factions within the party. This move effectively cut off the Mensheviks and other revolutionaries. However, he also admitted to all at the Congress that changes would be needed. He said, "We are indeed in need of changes. We must broaden the base of our government. We should introduce economic relaxations and concessions."[54]

FIRST ILLNESS

From the very beginning and through the revolution and civil war, Lenin had for all intents been the single head of every facet of the soviet government. Now as the ruler of a vast land in great economic and social difficulties, he had to delegate authority. He was aided—or in some cases obstructed—by four top officials: Stalin,

in charge of party administration; Trotsky, head of the military; Grigory Zinoviev, in charge of Petrograd; and Lev Kamenev, directing activities. Trotsky was generally distrusted by the other three because he had sided with the Mensheviks for a long time before joining the revolution. Although Lenin and Stalin got along well together in general, Stalin often challenged the leader openly, especially when it came to matters of party machinery.

For some time before the Eleventh Congress convened in March 1922, Lenin had not been feeling well. He complained of frequent headaches and dizziness. He could not sleep and was generally tired. His doctors assured him that he was suffering from overwork, but Lenin, who suddenly began to study medical books, only said, "I feel this is the first sign."[55] Indeed, the Eleventh Congress would be his last.

Perhaps, as it turned out, the most significant work of the Eleventh Congress was the appointment of Joseph Stalin to the position of general-secretary of the Communist Party. Already commissar for the nationalities and commissar for the workers' and peasants' inspectorate, Stalin now had tremendous power. Although Lenin did not suggest this promotion, he did approve it, so there is no indication of the later rift that would occur between the two men.

A month after the Congress, Lenin was examined by Moscow's leading medical specialists. They concluded that the bullet still lodged in his neck since the attempted assassination of 1918 was the cause of his medical problems, although Lenin had complained of headaches long before the shooting. An operation was successfully performed at Moscow's Soldatenkov Hospital on April 23. A small abscess had formed at the bullet site, causing the doctors to feel justified in their diagnosis. Lenin recovered quickly and went back to work.

However, little more than a month passed before Lenin suffered a massive stroke on May 25, 1922. It was later diagnosed as arteriosclerosis of the brain. Known more commonly as hardening of the arteries, arteriosclerosis generally involves the formation of fatty deposits, or plaque, in the vessels that cut off blood flow to the brain or other organs.

Grigory Zinoviev (left) and Lev Kamenev (right) were two of the top officials in Lenin's government. Together with Leon Trotsky and Joseph Stalin, they governed the country as Lenin's health declined.

According to a biographer, "The whole right side of his body was rendered immobile. He had difficulty speaking. His mind was confused; he was desperate. His recovery was obviously going to be long and uncertain."[56] In reality, he returned to work in October. He still needed assistance with walking, but he acted clear headed and in control.

BREAK WITH STALIN

In the meantime, during Lenin's illness, the power of the government was in the hands of three men—Stalin, Zinoviev, and

Kamenev, with Trotsky being pushed more and more out of leadership roles. The distrust escalated among all of them, but especially between Stalin and Trotsky. Stalin began to assert his authority. He issued a resolution in the fall of 1922 that enraged Lenin. It said the Russian Socialist Federative Soviet Republic (RSFSR), the section of the country that included Moscow and over which Lenin had direct control, was also in charge of the five other Socialist Soviet Republics (SSRs) that had been established during the first years of the revolution. Stalin's proposal to give the RSFSR control over the entire country violated Lenin's concept of equality among all soviets that Lenin saw as essential for the development of communism. At last, Lenin began to sense that Stalin was making an attempt to usurp as much power as he could and destroy the revolution's aims as Lenin saw them.

Seeing Stalin as a man with a thirst for power did not really surprise Lenin. Experts tend to agree that Lenin had always known Stalin was capable of great ruthlessness when it came to his own aims. But since Stalin had generally always sided with Lenin, he had been an important ally against Trotsky and other comrades. What perhaps Lenin did not realize was the extent to which Stalin was angered and challenged by him and other members of the central committee. They often and casually referred to Stalin as not

Lenin (left) recognized that Stalin (right) cared more about securing power than developing communism.

being intelligent. Said biographer Robert Service,

> Such a misperception of Stalin's mental capacities was common enough to the intellectuals of Bolshevism. The humiliation felt by Stalin reinforced his determination to wreak a terrible revenge on them when the opportunity came. He himself had always had ambitions as a theorist as well as an administrator, and evidently thought his writings on the national question to be a substantial contribution to a growing revolutionary corpus; and, while Stalin could not match the flashes of inspiration in the humanities and the social sciences displayed by Trotski and Bukharin, there is little in the work of Zinoviev, Kamenev, Poyatakov or any other outstanding Bolshevik politician which put them out of his intellectual class. And, quite apart from Stalin's qualities as a theorist, it was fatuous for Lenin to refer to him so casually as unintelligent.[57]

When Stalin had pushed to make the Russian Soviet dominant over the others, other members of the party agreed even though it violated the concept of equality. This made Lenin realize that the Bolshevik Party had become infected with what he called "Russian chauvinism." That was the idea that Russian was the dominant nationalism, that the other republics in the vast country, which were not all composed of ethnic Russians, were somehow inferior and meant to be dominated—exactly what tsarism had preached. Russian chauvinism had been present to some degree during Lenin's childhood, and he may have been especially sensitive to it since his own parents were not ethnic Russians.

Until Lenin recovered his strength and abilities, there was little he could do to curb the direction of his government. His sister Maria came to nurse him while Krupskaya helped him to speak distinctly once again and to write with his left hand. As before, Lenin was a serious student and dedicated. He was visited in August by Stalin, who reported that he acted much like his old self. Interestingly, Stalin was very careful not to show any ill will toward Lenin. As Wolfe states, "Stalin professes that until Lenin's death he was no more than Lenin's 'best and most faithful disciple.'"[58]

With almost superhuman effort, Lenin willed himself to recover enough to right the wrongs of his government and find the man or men capable of succeeding him. He knew that Stalin cared only for securing his own power, not for the cause of true communism. Then disaster struck again. On the night of December 22, 1922, Lenin suffered another stroke and was paralyzed on his right side.

A Political Testament

Unable to write and aware that recovery was near impossible, Lenin dictated what he called a political testament to his secretary during December 30 and 31. It was later read to the party Congress. As noted by biographer Clark, it began: "Comrade

SETTING AN EXAMPLE

Writer J.N. Westwood believes that Lenin's unscrupulousness and ruthlessness set an example for future leaders. This view is summed up in Russia: 1917–1964:

"Lenin was energetic, single-minded, and strong-willed. He also had a useful unscrupulousness in dealing with those who opposed him. This was not because he was ruthless and dishonest by nature, but because he was so certain of his own rightness that any means of assuring the victory of his ideas seemed justified, and in any case he had rejected much of conventional morality. (This ruthlessness subsequently became a hallmark of successful Communist leaders, including some who possessed few other qualities to excuse it.)"

Stalin, having become Secretary-General, has unlimited authority concentrated in his hands, and I am not sure whether he will always be capable of using that authority with sufficient caution."[59] Lenin went on to call Trotsky the most capable of the leaders at the top. Then he spoke of his main worry that a split in the party would result from the tensions between Stalin and Trotsky. He also discussed the qualities of the other leading officials in the party.

Lenin condemned Stalin in stronger terms in the postscript that he added to the political testament on January 4, 1923. He called Stalin "too rude" and said it was a defect that was not tolerable for someone holding the position of secretary-general. He suggested strongly that the comrades find a way to remove Stalin from the post and replace him with a more tolerant and loyal person. These at-tributes had assumed tremendous impor-tance to Lenin in the formation of the party and especially in the administration of the government.

For a short time after the political testa-ment, Lenin seemed to recover some of his enthusiasm. He even felt he was re-gaining the use of his arm. Some of his cheerfulness was the result of his having won a point with the central committee on the subject of foreign trade. The com-mittee agreed with Lenin's wishes that foreign trade must be strengthened and promoted.

However, his disagreement with and suspicions about Stalin remained. Feeling cut off from his authority and unable to battle his enemies as he had done before, Lenin instead dictated a note to Stalin on March 5, 1923. According to David Shub, it severed "all personal and comradely re-lations with Stalin."[60]

One of Lenin's major conflicts with Stalin during this period was over the province of Georgia, where Stalin was born. Relations between Russia and Georgia were regulated by treaty. Lenin and Stalin bitterly debated over whether to grant the region self-government or make it an integral part of the Soviet Union. Lenin wanted to create an independent unit that would have joined the Russian state. During these arguments, Lenin once again claimed that Stalin was extremely rude. This trait of rudeness in Stalin was a seemingly small matter that apparently agitated Lenin a great deal. Some historians believe that the frequent arguments and constant friction between the two men contributed to Lenin's deteriorating health.

THE END OF AN ERA

Lenin's break with Stalin and his suggestion to remove him from a position of power came too late to be meaningful, for later in March 1923, Lenin suffered his third stroke. This time he was left almost completely incapacitated and incapable of speaking. Yet his will, if not his health, was remarkable. In the middle of May he was taken to his home in Gorki away from the Kremlin, supposedly to spend his last days in comfort. By July he was out in the garden in a wheelchair and later walked across the room with the aid of a cane. According to his wife's journals, Lenin's interest in politics rebounded, although he was still unable

to speak beyond uttering partial words to make himself understood. In October, Lenin upset his wife and amazed his doctors by insisting that he be taken back to Moscow. According to reports, he returned to his office in the Kremlin and then was taken to his apartment where he spent the holidays.

During the month of January 1924, Lenin's health remained about the same, but he was in good spirits. Then, in the

In 1923 Lenin suffered a third stroke that briefly confined him to a wheelchair.

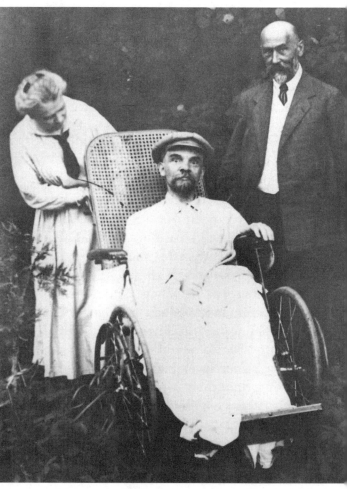

early morning hours of January 21, he suffered his final stroke. Lenin lapsed into a coma and died later in the day. According to Christopher Hill, comrade Mikhail Kalinin "wept when he announced the news to the Congress of the Soviets."[61]

The news of the leader's death came as quite a shock to the party members, since few of them had been told the extent of his illness. After an autopsy, which confirmed that he had died of a brain hemorrhage, Lenin's body was taken to Moscow where it lay until the following Saturday. Thousands of people lined the thirty-mile route from Gorki to Moscow as the train bearing his body passed, and hundreds of thousands filed by his coffin where it lay in the House of the Trade Unions. The only one of the soviet officials who did not attend the funeral was Trotsky. He had been away and later declared that the other leaders had not told him of the correct day for the funeral.

Although he had no religion during his life, Lenin was nearly canonized after his death. His body, unlike other revolutionary leaders, was not buried or cremated. The Communist Party, after much debate, decided to preserve his body as long as possible. Lenin was embalmed and put in a mausoleum in Red Square in August 1924.

Other tributes followed as the entire country seemed caught with emotion. In a ringing speech, Stalin declared that the party would carry on Lenin's fight for a Communist International throughout the world. The city of Petrograd immediately became Leningrad (it went back to its original name of St. Petersburg in 1991). The Sparrow Hills of Moscow were re-named Lenin Hills. His life and his achievements passed quickly into legend.

THE AFTERMATH

In the year following Lenin's death, Stalin led an extravagant campaign of near idolization of the fallen leader. At the same time he was promoting himself and soon had the city of Tsaritsyn changed to Stalingrad (it is now Volgograd). With the aid of Zinoviev and Kamenev, he was able to oust Trotsky from the seat of power. Soon after, he joined with Nikolay Bukharin and Aleksey Rykov in arranging the deaths of Zinoviev and Kamenev. Bukharin and Rykov eventually followed the others into political limbo, and when Stalin expelled Trotsky from the country in 1929 and later had him assassinated in Mexico, Stalin emerged as sole leader of the Soviet Union. Impatient with Lenin's idea of a world revolution, Stalin instead concentrated on a policy of "socialism in one country."

In all probability Lenin would have been enraged to learn that his successor, Joseph Stalin, became a dictator who exercised greater political power over the next twenty-five years than any other historical figure. A skilled but ruthless organizer, Stalin failed to promote Lenin's dream of a classless society, but he created a mighty industrial-military complex and led the Soviet Union into the nuclear age.

Lenin spent nearly all of his life in pursuit of one goal—socialist revolution at home and abroad—yet he spent less than six years as the leader of state in trying to

THE REMAINS OF LENIN

The lengthy lines to view the tomb of Lenin in Red Square have dropped off in recent years, and Red Square is now closed to visitors for three mornings a week. There is no longer an honor guard at the tomb's entrance; however, some of the curious still visit.

Lenin's mausoleum remains an impressive site. Designed by Alexei Shohusev in 1924, it is a red granite-faced pyramid highlighted with black labradorite. The talk through the years of moving the mausoleum out of the square because it is a reminder of the revolution's violence seems to have died down. For now, the former dictator remains in his crystal casket.

Lenin's tomb is located in a mausoleum in Red Square, Moscow.

reach that goal. He did not live to see the classless society of prosperity for all, and his dream of a world socialist revolution never came close to being realized. Yet, with whatever methods at his disposal and with bold, often ruthless determination, he brought socialism to his country. For good or ill, Lenin remains one the most important and unforgettable figures of any century.

It is impossible to say whether the history of the Soviet Union would have been different had Lenin survived his fifty-fourth birthday. Yet his impact on his country is undeniable. He was the architect and builder of the soviet state, the strongest Communist state in existence until that time. The Bolshevik Revolution has sometimes been called the most important political event of the twentieth century. If that is so, then Lenin as its spearhead should be regarded as the century's most important political leader. In any event, he was a unique personality who left a lasting mark upon his people.

Lenin was a man with a mission. Once he had grasped it, he never swayed from

LENIN AND STALIN

On February 25, 1956, Stalin's successor, Nikita Khrushchev, gave a speech that denounced Stalin's brutality. In this excerpt, Khrushchev points out contrasts between Stalin's rule and Lenin's:

"Lenin used severe methods only in the most necessary cases, when the exploiting classes were still in existence and were vigorously opposing the revolution, when the struggle for survival was decidedly assuming the sharpest forms, even including a civil war.

Stalin, on the other hand, used extreme methods and mass repressions at a time when the revolution was already victorious, when the Soviet state was strengthened, when the exploiting classes were already liquidated, and Socialist relations were touted solidly in all phases of national economy, when our party was politically consolidated and had strengthened itself both numerically and ideologically. It is clear that here Stalin showed in a whole series of cases his intolerance, his brutality, and his abuse of power. Instead of proving his political correctness and mobilizing the masses, he often chose the path of repression and physical annihilation, not only against actual enemies, but also against individuals who had not committed any crimes against the party and the Soviet Government. Here we see no wisdom but only a demonstration of the brutal force which had once so alarmed V.I. Lenin."

Lenin's successor, Joseph Stalin, became a ruthless dictator.

A statue of Lenin overlooks Lenin Square in Moscow. Lenin left a lasting mark on his people and his country.

his efforts to fulfill it. Through exiles and banishment within his own party, he quietly regrouped until the time was right to strike again. Without compassion or uncertainty and with rigid, fanatical determination, Lenin let nothing and no one stand in the way of his dream of a Soviet Russia.

Lenin interpreted the teachings of Karl Marx (which excited and enlightened him) and others to fit his own needs in his own time to fulfill his own beliefs. He was without doubt at times a cold and ruthless killer, but such events, if he dwelt upon them at all, would probably have given him little pause in his relentless pursuit. The reign of Red Terror, the brutal behavior of Cheka and the Red Guard, was to Lenin only the means to bring about a necessary end. And he would allow nothing to stand in the way of that end. He often remarked that very few world figures had gained or retained power by relying on polite methods. Such a determined sense of drive and the patience to see it through were probably Lenin's great traits as a political leader.

Almost in contrast to his political self was Lenin the man. Few historical figures have lived a private life of almost austerity. He disliked and avoided personal items that would associate him with wealth. He dressed unremarkably, ate unremarkably, and beyond hunting and chess, he seemed to exist only for the one single ambition of his life—the forming of Soviet Russia.

Lenin has become the enduring image of the now disbanded Soviet Union. He remains forever the symbol of the Communist state. Yet in Russia, his image is still changing. The reverence for the former leader has been diminishing. In 1997, Russian leader Boris Yeltsin went so far as to propose that Lenin's remains should now be buried and the mausoleum taken down. Said Yeltsin in a Moscow newspaper article in 1999, "He will be buried. The question is when."[62]

At his death Lenin would probably not have judged himself successful in his own eyes, for the soviet state was still to be secured in Russia and his dream of international revolution did not yet seem plausible. But it cannot be denied that Vladimir Ulyanov, the man called Lenin, changed the history of the world.

Notes

Chapter 1: A Middle-Class Youth

1. Leon Trotsky, *The Young Lenin*. New York: Doubleday, 1972, p. 76.
2. Quoted in Ronald W. Clark, *Lenin: A Biography*. New York: Harper, 1988, p. 11.
3. Quoted in Clark, *Lenin*, p. 11.
4. Robert Service, *Lenin: A Biography*. Cambridge, MA: Harvard University Press, pp. 29–30.
5. Harold Shukman, *Lenin & the Russian Revolution*. New York: Putnam's, 1967, p. 131.
6. Quoted in Christopher Hill, *Lenin and the Russian Revolution*. London: English Universities Press, 1972, p. 36.
7. Quoted in Dmitri Volkogonov, *Lenin: A New Biography*. New York: Simon & Schuster, 1994, p. 19.
8. Quoted in Volkogonov, *Lenin*, p. 19.

Chapter 2: The Making of a Revolutionary

9. David Shub, *Lenin, a Biography*, New York: Country Life Press, 1948, p. 24.
10. Bertram D. Wolfe, *Three Who Made a Revolution*. New York: Dell, 1964, p. 109.
11. Seweryn Bialer, "Marx Had It Wrong. Does Gorbachev?" *U.S. News & World Report*, October 19, 1987, 103:41(1).
12. Wolfe, *Three Who Made a Revolution*, p. 90.
13. Service, *Lenin: A Biography*, p. 92.
14. C.M. Lloyd, "Lenin's Legacy," *New Statesman*, November 29, 1999, 128:45.
15. Quoted in Clark, *Lenin*, p. 33.
16. Service, *Lenin: A Biography*, p. 100.
17. Quoted in Hill, *Lenin and the Russian Revolution*, p. 38.
18. Quoted in Service, *Lenin: A Biography*, p. 117.

Chapter 3: Exile

19. Quoted in Robert Payne, *The Life and Death of Lenin*. New York: Simon & Schuster, 1964, p. 111.
20. Quoted in Clark, *Lenin*, p. 45.
21. Wolfe, *Three Who Made a Revolution*, p. 141.
22. Service, *Lenin, a Biography*, p. 123.
23. Quoted in Clark, *Lenin*, p. 54.
24. Payne, *The Life and Death of Lenin*, p. 135.

Chapter 4: The Rise of the Bolsheviks

25. Quoted in Clark, *Lenin*, p. 60.
26. Quoted in Shukman, *Lenin & the Russian Revolution*, p. 96.
27. Hill, *Lenin and the Russian Revolution*, p. 40.
28. Payne, *The Life and Death of Lenin*, pp. 170–71.
29. Shukman, *Lenin & the Russian Revolution*, p. 55.
30. Quoted in Clark, *Lenin*, p. 70.
31. Shukman, *Lenin & the Russian Revolution*, p. 92.

Chapter 5: The Aftermath of Bloody Sunday

32. Quoted in Shub, *Lenin*, p. 102.
33. Quoted in Hill, *Lenin and the Russian Revolution*, p. 161.
34. Quoted in Volkogonov, *Lenin*, p. 85.
35. Quoted in Shub, *Lenin*, p. 83.
36. Quoted in Shub, *Lenin*, p. 86.
37. Quoted in Volkogonov, *Lenin*, p. 56.
38. Quoted in Shub, *Lenin*, p. 107.
39. Quoted in Shub, *Lenin*, p. 108.
40. Richard Pipes, *Russia Under the Bolshevik Regime*. New York: Knopf, 1993, pp. 250–51.

Chapter 6: War and Revolution

41. Pipes, *Russia and the Bolshevik Regime*, p. 270.
42. Volkogonov, *Lenin*, p. 67.
43. Quoted in Clark, *Lenin*, p. 271.
44. Theodore von Laue, "A Perspective on History: The Soviet System Reconsidered," *The Historian*, Winter 1999, 61(i2):383.

Chapter 7: The All-Powerful Revolutionary

45. Gennadii Bordvogov, "The Policy and Regime of Extraordinary Measures in Russia under Lenin and Stalin," *Europe-Asia Studies*, June 1995, 47(4):5.
46. Shub, *Lenin*, p. 318.
47. Quoted in Volkogonov, *Lenin*, p. 207.
48. Quoted in Shub, *Lenin*, p. 303.
49. Quoted in Clark, *Lenin*, p. 370.
50. Robert Service, *Lenin: A Political Life.* Bloomington: Indiana University Press, 1995, p. 30.
51. Service, *Lenin: A Political Life*, p. 33.
52. Pipes, *Russia*, pp. 370–71.
53. Eugene D. Genovese, "The Unknown Lenin: From the Secret Archive," *The New Republic*, October 14, 1996, 215(16):49.

Chapter 8: The Last Years

54. Quoted in Clark, *Lenin*, p. 433.
55. Quoted in Shub, *Lenin*, p. 375.
56. Service, *Lenin: A Biography*, pp. 443–44.
57. Service, *Lenin: A Political Life*, p. 273.
58. Wolfe, *Three Who Made a Revolution*, p. 467.
59. Quoted in Clark, *Lenin*, p. 472.
60. Shub, *Lenin*, p. 382.
61. Hill, *Lenin and the Russian Revolution*, p. 153.
62. Quoted in "A Christian Burial for Lenin?" *Christian Century*, August 11, 1999, 166(122):769.

For Further Reading

Books

William Barbour, ed., *The Breakup of the Soviet Union.* San Diego: Greenhaven Press, 1994. A look at the factors that caused the disintegration of the great soviet state.

Hugh Brewster, *Anastasia's Album.* New York: Hyperion, 1996. A look at the mystery and legend surrounding Anastasia, the tsar's youngest daughter.

John Hainey, *Vladimir Ilich Lenin.* New York: Chelsea, 1988. A readable account of the founder of the soviet state.

Michael Kort, *The Rise and Fall of the Soviet Union.* New York: Watts, 1992. Historical events depicting what brought about the beginning and end of the Soviet Union.

David Pietrusza, *The End of the Cold War.* San Diego: Lucent, 1995. Focuses on the personalities and events that caused the friction between the Soviet Union and the United States.

Nancy Whitelaw, *Joseph Stalin: From Peasant to Premier.* New York: Dillon, 1992. The life and times of Russia's brutal dictator.

Websites

Alexander Palace (www.alexanderpalace.org). Describes everyday life in the Romanov palace and offers virtual tours. Contains biographies of past inhabitants, including tsars and their families.

Geographia (www.geographia.com). Provides information about and tours of several well-known cities, waterways, and buildings, such as the Kremlin.

Lenin Library (www.marx2mao.org). A collection of Lenin's work from 1893 to 1923; also has links to articles by Marx, Engels, and Stalin.

Works Consulted

Books

Ronald W. Clark, *Lenin: A Biography*. New York: Harper, 1988. A full-length biography using a complex historical record to shape the character of one of the most powerful figures of the twentieth century.

Anne Commire, ed., *Historic World Leaders*. Detroit: Gale, 1994. A reference set with articles on various leaders, including Lenin.

Christopher Hill, *Lenin and the Russian Revolution*. London: English Universities, 1972. One of a series of books that explores humankind and their times.

I.E. Levine, *Lenin, the Man Who Made a Revolution*. New York: Messner, 1969. Concentrates on the revolutionary activities of Lenin's life.

Robert Payne, *The Life and Death of Lenin*. New York: Simon & Schuster, 1964. A standard biography of the soviet leader.

Richard Pipes, *Russia Under the Bolshevik Regime*. New York: Knopf, 1993. Covers the outbreak of civil war until Lenin's death.

Leonard Schapiro and Peter Reddaway, eds., *Lenin, the Man, the Theorist, the Leader: A Reappraisal*. New York: Praeger, 1967. A book that concentrates on the philosophy and tactics of Lenin.

Robert Service, *Lenin: A Biography*. Cambridge, MA: Harvard University Press, 2000. A study of the revolutionary and the private man.

———, *Lenin: A Political Life: Vol. 3 The Iron Ring*. Bloomington, Indiana University Press, 1995. Covers Lenin from 1918 until his death.

David Shub, *Lenin, a Biography*. New York: Country Life Press, 1948. A biography full of conversations with and about Lenin.

Harold Shukman, *Lenin & the Russian Revolution*. New York: Putnam's, 1967. A concise history of the revolutionary movement in Russia.

Leon Trotsky, *The Young Lenin*. New York: Doubleday, 1972. By another dedicated revolutionary, a book concentrating on Lenin's early years.

Dmitri Volkogonov, *Lenin: A New Biography*. New York: Simon & Schuster, 1994. A biography of the revolutionary leader using the latest archival material.

Bertram D. Wolfe, *Three Who Made a Revolution*. New York: Dell, 1964. The revolutionary history of Lenin, Trotsky, and Stalin.

Periodicals

Seweryn Bialer, "Marx Had It Wrong. Does Gorbachev?" *U.S. News & World Report*, October 19, 1987, 103:41(1).

Chris Bryant, "Remains of the Deity," *New Statesman*, August 8, 1997, 126(4346):17.

Christian Century, "A Christian Burial for Lenin?" August 11, 1999, 16(i22):769.

Charles Fenyvesi, "The Communist Cult of the Dead," *U.S. News & World Report*, July 21, 1997, 123(n3):12(1).

David Filipow, "Yeltsin's Flair for Dramatic Served Him Well," *Boston Globe*, January 1, 2000.

Eugene D. Genovese, "The Unknown Lenin: From the Secret Archive," *The New Republic*, October 14, 1996, 215(16):49(5).

Andrew J. Glass, "Lenin's New Apostle," *The New Leader*, February 24, 1986, 69:3.

Jeffrey Heft, "Democracy's False Friend," *Wall Street Journal*, May 11, 1999, A20.

Andrew Higgins, "Getting Inside Lenin's Head," *World Press Review*, January 1994, 41(1):42.

The Historian, "The Collapse of the Lenin Personality Cult in Soviet Russia, 1985–1995," Winter 1998, 60(2): 325–44.

Robin Knight, "Communism Is Dead; Now Who Will Restore Decency?" *U.S. News & World Report*, July 23, 1990, 109(4):10(2).

Keszek Kolakowski, "Lenin Lives! The Lenin Cult in Soviet Russia," *New Republic*, June 4, 1983, 189:33–35.

Theodore von Laue, "A Perspective on History: The Soviet System Reconsidered," *The Historian*, Winter 1999, 61(i2):383.

C.M. Lloyd, "Lenin's Legacy," *New Statesman*, November 29, 1999, 128: 45.

Thomas M. Nichols, "Unreal Notions about Russia," *Boston Globe*, July 24, 2000, A17.

Trevor J. Smith, "The Collapse of the Lenin Personality Cult in Soviet Russia," *The Historian*, Winter 1998, 60(2):325.

Time, "Who Should be the Person of the Century?" Letter to the editor, August 30, 1999. 154(i9):17.

Mortimer B. Zuckerman, "Lenin's Dream Gone Beserk," *U.S. News & World Report*, March 7, 1988, 104(9):78(1).

Index

administrative exiles.
See exiles
Alexander II (tsar)
assassination of, 21
reforms of, 15, 18, 19
Alexander III (tsar), 15, 17
Alexandra (tsarina), 32, 66
aliases, 39, 41–42, 45, 47
All-Russian Bolshevik
Conference, 59
All-Russian Extraordinary
Commission for
Combating
Counterrevolution and
Sabotage, 74
Anastasia (princess), 81
Anderson, Anna, 81
Autopsy for an Empire: The
Seven Leaders Who Built
the Soviet Regime
(Volkogonov), 45, 72
Axelrod, Paul, 45

Bahdrt, Carl Friedrich, 75
Bernstein, Eduard, 40
Black Hundreds, 58
Black Night, White Snow
(Salisbury), 19
Black Repartition, 21
Blank, Moshe (great-
grandfather), 16
Bloody Sunday, 53–55, 56
Bolshevik Revolution. *See*
Russian Revolution
Bolsheviks
All-Russian Conference
of, 59
arrested by Kerensky, 70

control of Petrograd
Soviet of Workers' and
Soldiers' Deputies, 71
development of, 46, 52
opposition to Lenin by,
61, 69
renamed Communists,
68
RSDWP and
control of, 60, 63
Third Congress of, 55
Fourth Congress of, 59
two-stage revolution
philosophy of, 67
bourgeoisie
defined by Lenin, 52
in Marxism, 25
role of, in revolution, 37,
40, 67
Bronstein, Lev Davidovich.
See Trotsky, Leon
Brussels, 48–49
Bukharin, Nikolay, 94

capitalism
in Marxism, 13, 25
New Economic Policy
and, 85
peasants and, 31
reform of, 40
tsarist system and, 39–40
in two-stage revolution,
26
Catherine the Great, 20
Cheka, 74, 80, 82
Chernyshevsky, Nikolay
Gavrilovich, 19, 24
civil rights

Alexander III and, 17
Kronstadt rebellion and,
86
Lenin and, 74
Nicholas II and, 57, 58
civil war
Allies involvement in, 78
conditions leading to,
77–78
effects of, 84
execution of Nicholas II
and family during,
79–80, 81
leadership of Lenin
during, 78–79
Clark, Ronald, 91–92
class system
Lenin and, 26, 52
socialism and, 26
Clausewitz, Carl von, 24
colonialism, 12
communism, 13, 25
socialism and, 26
see also war communism
Communist International,
86
Communist League, 26
Communist Manifesto, The
(Marx and Engels), 27
Communist Party, 63, 68
Condition of the Working
Class in England, The
(Engels), 27
Council of People's
Commissars, 73
Critical Notes on the
Economic Development of
Russia (Struve), 40

Das Kapital (Marx), 27
Development of Capitalism in Russia (Lenin), 34, 39
Dostoyevsky, Fyodor, 35
dual-power concept, 69
Dumas
    Nicholas II and, 55, 60
    reorganized as Provisional Committee of the Duma, 66
Dzerzhinski, Feliks Edmundovich, 82

Economic and Philosophical Manuscripts (Marx), 27
Ekaterinburg, 79
Eleventh Congress of RSDWP, 88–89
Engels, Friedrich, 27–28
Evolutionary Socialism (Bernstein), 40
exiles, 35
    of Anna (sister), 21
    of Dmitri (brother), 34
    of Krupskaya, 37, 42–43, 47
    of Lenin
        to Kokushkino, 23
        to Siberia, 34–40, 42, 44
    of Maria (sister), 34
    of members of Union for the Struggle for the Liberation of the Working Class, 35
    of Nicholas II and family, 70–71
    of RSDWP Duma members, 60
    of Stalin, 63
    of Trotsky, 50

famine, 28, 77, 84

Fifth Congress of RSDWP, 60
Finland, 59, 60
Fourth Congress of RSDWP, 59
Frey, 45

Gapon, George, 53, 56
Geneva
    Lenin in, 47–48, 62
    Third Congress of RSDWP in, 55
Georgia, 93
German Social Democratic Party, 40
Gil, S.K., 83
Gorky, Maksim, 87

Hermitage, 20
Hill, Christopher
    on Lenin, 34, 47, 94
Historian (journal), 76
History of Trade Unionism (Sidney and Beatrice Webb), 39
House of Preliminary Detention, 34
House of the Dead, The (Dostoyevsky), 35
How I "Discovered" Religion in Russia (Lazzari), 74

Ilin, Vladimir, 39
Industrial Revolution, 12, 31
International Socialist Bureau, 64
Iskra (newspaper), 44–46, 47, 51–52

Jewish Workers' Alliance, 40

Kalinin, Mikhail, 94

Kamenev, Lev
    in soviet government, 88, 90
    Stalin and, 94
Kaplan, Fanya, 83–84
Kautsky, Karl, 24
Kazan University, 21–22
Kerensky, Aleksandr
    arrest of Bolsheviks by, 70
    attempted comeback by, 73
    escape of, 72
    Lenin and, 71
    in provisional government, 66–67
    World War I and, 69, 70
Kerensky, Fyodor, 21
Khrushchev, Nikita, 96
Kokushkino, 21, 23, 24
Krasnoyarsk, 36
Kremlin, 78
Kronstadt rebellion, 85–86
Krupskaya, Nadezhda Konstantinovna (wife Nadya)
    appearance of, 30–31
    background of, 30
    exile of, 37, 42–43, 47
    illness of Lenin and, 91
    importance of, to Lenin's work, 39
    in London, 47
    marriage, 30, 31, 37–39
    return of, during Revolution of 1905, 57

Land and Freedom, 46
law practice, 29
    class bias in, 27
    in Siberia, 39
Lazzari, Aldo Quinto, 74

Lenin
  on abolition of churches,
    58
  aliases of, 39, 41–42, 45, 47
  appearance of
    as child, 14
    as man, 28, 48, 67
  assassination attempt on,
    82–84
  attitude of, toward
    World War I, 65
  boyhood of, 15, 16
  characteristics of
    charisma, 29, 67, 69
    frugality, 31
    ruthlessness, 92
    self-confidence, 15
  death of, 94
  death of father and, 17, 18
  education of
    ability as student, 12,
      15
    early, 14
    at Kazan University,
      21, 22–23
    law, 26–27
  European journey of, 31,
    33
  family of, 14, 16
  on financing revolution,
    61–62
  health of
    chronic illnesses, 31
    in Paris, 62
    after revolution, 88, 89
    during Second
      Congress, 51
    in Siberia, 39
    stress and, 47–48, 53
    strokes, 89–90, 91,
      93–94
  importance of, 12, 95, 97

  imprisonment of, 33–34
  marriage of, 30, 31, 37–39
  nickname of, 14
  political testament of,
    91–92
  recreational activities of,
    17, 39, 97
  remains of, 94, 95
  tactics of, 45, 48–49, 92,
    96
Lenin: A Biography
  (Service), 26, 62
Leningrad, 20, 94
Life and Death of Lenin, The
  (Payne), 86
London, 47

Martov, V.O.
  disagreement with Lenin
    over party structure,
    50–52
  Iskra and, 45
  in London, 47
  secret police and, 44
Marx, Karl Heinrich, 13,
  24, 27
Marxism
  described, 13, 24–25
  effect of, on Lenin, 25–26
  modified by Lenin, 37
Mensheviks
  development of, 46, 52
  Lenin's opinion of, 59
  provisional government
    and, 66, 67–68
  RSDWP and, 88
    Third Congress of, 55
    Fourth Congress of, 59
  St. Petersburg Soviet of
    Workers' Deputies
    and, 57
Mexico, 50

Mikhail (grand duke), 80
Moscow, 20, 59, 77
mutinies, 56, 85–86

New Economic Policy
  (NEP), 85
New Life (magazine), 57–58
New Republic (magazine), 86
New Statesman (magazine),
  29
Nicholas I (tsar), 15, 20
Nicholas II (tsar)
  abdication of, 67, 69
  abilities of, 53–54
  background of, 32
  characteristics of, 32
  civil rights and, 57, 58
  Dumas and, 55, 60
  execution of, 79–80, 81
  exile of, 70–71

Okhrana, 33
"One Step Forward, Two
  Steps Back" (Lenin),
  52–53
"On the National Pride of
  the Great Russians"
  (Lenin), 45
On War (Clausewitz), 24

Paris, 62
Payne, Robert
  on Kronstadt rebellion, 86
  on Lenin in Siberia, 43
peasants
  Black Repartition and, 21
  civil war and, 77, 79
  famine and aid to, 28
  Lenin as lawyer for, 27
  New Economic Policy
    and, 85
  number of, 29

role of, in revolution, 29,
31, 37, 46
war communism and,
84–85
People's Freedom, 21
Peter I (Peter the Great), 20
Petrograd, 20
abandoned by Lenin, 77
renaming of, 94
Soviet of Workers' and
Soldiers' Deputies, 66
Bolshevik control of, 71
dual power and, 69
overthrow of
provisional
government by, 72
strikes in, 66
Petrov, 45
Pipes, Richard
on Lenin, 65, 67
on war communism, 84
Plekhanov, Georgy
Valentinovich, 46
alias of, 42
Lenin and, 33, 39–40,
44–45, 47
RSDWP structure and,
51, 52
two-stage revolution
philosophy of, 26
Potemkin (cruiser), 56
Potrezov, Alexander, 44–45,
45
Prague, 63
Pravda (newspaper), 63, 64
Proletarian (newspaper), 62
proletariat
Bloody Sunday and, 53,
54, 56
civil war and, 77, 79
importance of, to Lenin,
29

in Marxism, 25
role in revolution of, 37,
40, 67
size of, 29
Provisional Committee of
the Duma, 66
provisional government
formation of, 66–67
Lenin and, 67–68
overthrow of, 71–72
Plekhanov and, 46
popular support for, 70
Soviets and dual-power
concept and, 69
Pskov, 44

Rasputin, 66
Red Guards, 71–72
Reed, John, 72
religion
atheism of Lenin, 17
boyhood, 16
proposed abolition of
churches, 58
under soviet
government, 74
revolution
early organizations
promoting, 21, 28–29
financing, 59, 61–62
importance of, to Lenin,
49
in Marxism, 25
philosophers of
Bernstein, 40
Chernyshevsky, 19, 24
Clausewitz, 24
Kautsky, 24
Marx, 24–26
Plekhanov, 26
Struve, 40–41
two-stage, 26, 37, 40, 67

world, 65, 86–87
Revolution of 1905
agitation by Lenin
during, 55–56
Bloody Sunday, 53–55, 56
return of Lenin, 57
Soviets during, 57–59
strikes and, 55, 57, 58–59
Richter, Jacob, 47
Romanov, House of, 15, 81
Russia
conditions in, after
abdication of Nicholas
II, 69
early history of, 22
Industrial Revolution in,
31
trade unions in, 63
during World War I,
65–66
Russia: 1917–1964
(Westwood), 92
Russian chauvinism, 91
Russian Revolution
beginning of, 66
importance of, 95
provisional government
and
formation of, 66–67
Lenin and, 67–68
overthrow of, 71–72
Plekhanov and, 46
popular support for, 70
soviets and
importance of, 68
see also Petrograd,
Soviet of Workers'
and Soldiers'
Deputies, 66
Russian Social Democratic
Workers' Party (RSDWP)
Bolshevik control of, 63

division of, 46
exile of Duma members
of, 60
founding of, 40
newspaper of, 44–46, 47,
51–52
opposition to Lenin by
Bolsheviks in, 61
see also specific congresses
Russian Social Democrats,
40
Russian Socialist Federative
Soviet Republic (RSFSR),
78, 90, 91
Russo-Japanese War, 53
Rykov, Aleksey, 94

Salisbury, Harrison, 19
Schanzkowski, Franziska, 81
Second Congress of
RSDWP
in Brussels, 48–49
in London, 49–52
secret police
under Lenin, 74, 80, 82
under tsars, 29, 33, 42, 44
Semenevsky Guards, 59
serfs, 18–19
see also peasants
Service, Robert
on Lenin, 26, 62, 84
on Stalin, 91
Shohusev, Alexei, 95
Shub, David, 92
Shukman, Harold
on founding of Vperyod,
53
on Lenin, 17, 50
on *What Is To Be Done?*, 47
Shuskenskoye, 36–37
Siberia, 41
strike by miners in, 63

Simbirsk, 14, 16
Sinyavski, Andrei, 52
socialism, 19, 21, 26
aid to peasants and, 28
evolution into, 40–41
World War I and, 65
Socialist Democratic Party,
24
Socialist International
Congress, 62–63
Socialist Soviet Republics
(SSR), 90
*Soviet Civilization: A
Cultural History*
(Sinyavski), 52
soviet government
conditions faced by,
77–78
early measures by Lenin,
73–74
elections for, 74–75
formation of, 73
religion under, 74
top officials of, 88
Soviets
described, 57
equality among, 90
Revolution of 1905 and,
57–59
Russian Revolution
(1917) and
importance of, 68
see also Petrograd,
Soviet of Workers'
and Soldiers'
Deputies, 66
Stalin, Joseph
attempt of, to usurp
power, 90
became leader, 50
Bukharin and, 94
characteristics of, 90–91,

93, 96
Eleventh Congress of
RSDWP and, 88–89
exile of, 63
Kamenev and, 94
Khrushchev's
denunciation of, 96
Lenin and, 59, 71, 91–93
methods of, 96
Rykov and, 94
in soviet government, 73,
88, 90
Tiflis holdup and, 61
Trotsky and, 94
Zinoviev and, 94
State and Revolution
(Lenin), 70
Stockholm, 59
Stolypin, Pyotr
Arkadyevich, 60, 63
St. Petersburg, 20
House of Preliminary
Detention in, 34
revolutionary
organizations in, 28–29
Revolution of 1905 in,
53–59
see also Petrograd
strikes
by miners in Siberia, 63
Revolution of 1905 and,
57, 58–59
Russian Revolution
(1917) and, 66
Struve, Pyotr
Berngardovich, 40–41
Switzerland, 65

Tass, 63
Tenth Congress of RSDWP,
88
terrorism, 21, 80, 82

Third Congress of RSDWP, 55

Third International, 86

Three Who Made a Revolution (Wolfe), 25

Tiflis holdup, 61

"To the Citizens of Russia" (Lenin), 72–73

trade unions, 63

Trans-Siberian Railway, 41

Treaty of Brest-Litovsk, 75–76

Trotsky, Leon
on abilities of Lenin, 14
exiles of, 50
Lenin's opinion of, 92
in London, 47
peace treaty and, 75–76
Petrograd Soviet of Workers' and Soldiers' Deputies and, 71
return of, to Russia, 70
in soviet government, 73, 88, 90
Stalin and, 94
St. Petersburg Soviet of Workers' Deputies and, 57

tsarist system, 12–13, 15
capitalism and, 39–40
class bias in, 26
divine absolutism of tsar, 32
secret police in, 29, 33, 42, 44

two-stage revolution, 26, 37, 40, 67

Ufa, 42

Ulyanov, Alexander (brother Sasha)

arrest of, 18
death of father and, 17–18
execution of, 21
influence of, on Lenin, 17
revolution and, 18, 19

Ulyanov, Anna (sister)
arrest of, 18
exile of, 21
imprisonment of Lenin and, 34

Ulyanov, Dmitri (brother), 34

Ulyanov, Ilich Nikolayevich (father), 14, 16, 17

Ulyanov, Maria Alexandrovna (mother)
Alexander and, 19
background of, 14, 16
death of, 68–69
health of, 34
Lenin and, 21, 23, 34
as new Russian, 17

Ulyanov, Maria (sister), 34, 91

Ulyanov, Vladimir Ilich. *See* Lenin

Union for the Struggle for the Liberation of the Working Class
exile of members of, 35
formation of, 29
Okhrana and, 33

Union of Soviet Socialist Republics, 22

U.S. News & World Report (magazine), 25

Vasilyev, Mikhail, 56–57

Vladimir (grand duke), 54

Volgin, 42

Volkagonov, Dmitri
on Lenin, 45, 72

Vperyod (newspaper), 53

V.U.I., 45

war communism, 84–85

Webb, Beatrice, 39

Webb, Sidney, 39

Westwood, J.N.
on Lenin, 37, 92

What Is To Be Done? (Chernyshevsky), 24

What Is To Be Done? (Lenin), 47

White Army, 77, 78

Wolfe, Bertram
on stages of Marxism, 25
on Stalin, 91

workers. *See* proletariat

Workers' Cause, (newspaper), 52

World War I
armistice, 73
attitude of Lenin toward, 65
beginning of, 65
Kerensky and, 69, 70
peace treaty, 75–76
Russia during, 65–66

World War II, 20

Zasulich, Vera, 44
Iskra and, 45
in London, 47

Zhenka (dog), 39

Zinoviev, Grigory
in soviet government, 88, 90
Stalin and, 94

Zinoviev, Stepan, 62

Picture Credits

Cover image: © Bettmann/CORBIS
© Bettmann/CORBIS, 28, 49, 69, 82, 83
© Corel, 20, 78, 95, 97
© Historical Picture Archive/CORBIS, 80
© Hulton Archive by Getty Images, 36, 38, 51, 56, 60, 61, 68, 71, 81, 89 (left and right), 90, 93
© Hulton-Deutsch Collection/CORBIS, 13, 15, 16, 30
© Image Select/Art Resource, NY, 25
Chris Jouan, 33
© Erich Lessing/Art Resource, NY, 73
North Wind Picture Archives, 18, 22, 32, 85
© Snark/Art Resource, NY, 96

About the Authors

Corinne J. Naden, a former U.S. Navy journalist and children's book editor, has authored almost eighty books for young readers. She lives in Tarrytown, New York.

Rose Blue has published some eighty fiction and nonfiction books for children, two of which were adapted and aired by the NBC television network. A native New Yorker, she resides in Brooklyn.